FUELED BY
GREATNESS

10 Cutting Edge Strategies for Accelerating Your Destiny Now!

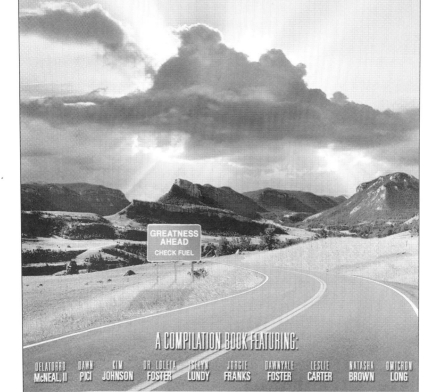

GREATNESS
AHEAD
CHECK FUEL

A COMPILATION BOOK FEATURING:

| DELATORRO McNEAL, II | DAWN PICI | KIM JOHNSON | DR. LOLETA FOSTER | ISLETA LUNDY | JORGIE FRANKS | DAWNYALE FOSTER | LESLIE CARTER | NATASHA BROWN | OMICRON LONG |

Foreword by Willie Jolley, CSP, CPAE
Author of the International Bestseller, A Setback Is a Setup for a Comeback!

Library of Congress Catalog Card Number: Pending

ISBN: 0-9721324-6-5

Bulk rate discounted purchasing is available by contacting the author you originally purchased your book from. See individual chapters for contact information.

Editing: Robin M. Boylorn, Delatorro McNeal, II, and Chapter Authors
All Graphic Design: Bill York, York Illustration and Design, Inc.
Printing: A&A Printing, Inc.

First Edition

10 9 8 7 6 5 4 3 2 1

Dedication

This book is lovingly dedicated to **YOU**, the reader, for making a quality decision to pursue your greatness and to **Delatorro McNeal, II,** with appreciation.

Delatorro, thank you. . .

"for being a ball of energy. . ."

"for having contagious enthusiasm for life. . ."

"for seeing something in us that we didn't see in ourselves. . ."

"for doing to us what we aspire to do for others: empowering and encouraging us to go farther, faster and higher than we would have without you."

When greatness is shared, it is multiplied. When greatness is multiplied, the world becomes a better place to live. Thank you for making the world a better place to live.

We honor you for your mentorship and your friendship.

-Fueled by Greatness Authors

Table of Contents

Forward by Willie Jolley

What is greatness? Some would say it's the ultimate achievement of one's highest and most worthwhile goal. Others would say it's a level of attainment in life, where a person feels as though they have reached a level of mastery of their craft, gift, talent, ability, or skill. Yet others would say that greatness is raising great children, in a challenging world. Moreover, some would define greatness as being the first in their family to graduate college. Still others would perhaps say that greatness is making it in Hollywood, or being a celebrity, or becoming rich and famous. While all of these definitions are well and good, I would like to submit to you that greatness is much simpler than that.

You see, I believe that greatness is a student who started out failing school, and then got inspired to unleash the genius within, and comeback from that academic setback, and make great grades. That is greatness. I believe that greatness is that parent (single or married) who makes the commitment to raise their child with the best of love, time, attention, affection, living, and learning that is possible to make that child a great citizen and contributor to this world. That is greatness. **I believe that greatness is the school teacher, who is underpaid for the outstanding difference that he or she makes on students' lives everyday in the classroom. That is greatness. I believe that greatness is the difference between what you are doing and what you could be doing and simply closing the gap!** George Washington Carver said that *"Greatness is not so much what you become, but what you have to overcome in the process!"* **It is anyone who commits their life to being the best they can be, sharing their great gifts and talents with this world, and leaving this world and every life they touched in the process, better than the way they found it.**

Now, when you are *Fueled by Greatness* I believe you are fueled from two directions. **First, you are fueled by the vision of what you see in your wonderful future. But in order to be driven by what you see in your tomorrow, you must create a compelling future that beckons to you and calls you to action on a daily basis.** In other words, you are fueled by the destination. Because you see a greater you in your tomorrow than you see today, you are fueled by the desire to become that greater individual. **Secondly, you are fueled by the desire to grow yourself and your impact. Each and every person on this earth is fueled by something or someone.** Some are fueled by the pursuit of money, riches, fame, and bling bling. Others are fueled by the desire to make a difference, leave a legacy, change a generation, and duplicate their life lessons into the lives of other people. The goal is to be fueled by the greatness of great people, and by the vision that people of greatness help you create for yourself in your present and future.

I can recall a time when I as preparing to speak for a group of students, and I was asking a young man if he was planning to come to my presentation. He replied back to me, "*Yeah, but only once you tell me what kind of car you drive.*" I was surprised by his comment, but was going to answer, because I do drive a nice car. However, before responding to his question, I thought to myself. You know, in truth, it really should not matter to this young man what I drive, what should matter is what drives me. **Because if I could teach him the things that drive, that fuel, that propel, that ignite, that engage me, he can drive any vehicle he wants.** In this materialistic society that we live in today, many people are focused on bling bling, rather than the main thing. **You see, it doesn't matter what successful people drive, what really matters is what DRIVES successful people!**

I remember when Delatorro asked me to be one of his professional mentors in the speaking and publishing industry five short years ago. Today, he has not only built a very successful speaking and publishing business, but he also teaches his greatness to others, hence this compilation book, *Fueled by Greatness.* **You see, when you have been fueled by great people, you can't help but to pass that greatness along and fuel others.**

In this amazing book, you will have the wonderful opportunity to learn what I call TIPS (Techniques, Ideas, Principles and Strategies) that Delatorro and his team of nine speakers, trainers, and authors have compiled just for you. Once internalized, processed and applied these tips will literally shave years off your learning and development curve and help you to accelerate your destiny. *Wouldn't you like to get where you really want to be in life, faster? Wouldn't you like to turbo charge your business, family, career, attitude, health, goals, and overall wellbeing?* I know you do, because we all do. I challenge you to **not only read this book, anybody can do that, but make a commitment to experience this book,** and use it as a roadmap to help facilitate your journey to success. **Live what you learn,** and you will indeed collapse the time it takes for you to fulfill your greatness. God Bless.

Willie Jolley, CSP, CPAE
Award Winning Speaker, Singer, Best Selling Author and Media Personality
www.WillieJolley.com
Phone: 202-723-8863 /800-487-8899

DELATORRO'S DYNAMIC DESTINY DOZEN

First and foremost, congratulations for making the quality decision to invest in your greatness by purchasing this book. If you did not purchase this book and it was given to you as a gift, then congratulations for committing to digest the plethora of powerful information, wisdom, and empowerment this book contains. I am very proud of you for doing so and excited to share with you what I believe to be some of the most cutting edge information about destiny acceleration that exists today. So let's go for it.

The purpose of this book is to teach you, coach you, and empower you to accelerate your destiny and help others around you do the same. My goal in this chapter is to cut your learning and development curve by teaching you the exact steps that I took, take, and will continue to take to not only pursue, but powerfully apprehend my destiny.

For the past decade I have dedicated my life to the study of human achievement, the psychology of success, and the fulfillment of purpose and destiny. Having made a global impact upon the world through speaking engagements, television, radio, and the internet I have seen and studied the best of the best. I have formal as well as self-taught education and training, and I have learned a tremendous amount about life that I would like to now download to you. If you are ready to install some new success software, then keep reading.

There is a difference between **the good and the great.**
There is a difference between **the ordinary and the extraordinary.**
There is a difference between **the dream livers & dream dreamers.**
There is a difference between **the wealthy and the destitute.**

What is that difference you may be asking?
THE PRICE THAT WAS PAID!

The "above average" pay a different price than "the average!" **They make a lifetime commitment to next level living and make their greatness and success mandatory.**

Now please understand something, when I talk about greatness I am not talking about fame. If you have read any of my previous books you know that everyone that's famous is not great, and everyone that's great is not famous! True greatness exists within all of us, it is simply a matter of unearthing and extracting that which is hidden deep within us on a daily basis.

Friend, please hear me. **You have within your being the power to speed up or slow down your greatness,** your destiny, your success, your next level, your abundance, your prosperity, your fulfillment in life, your wealth, your health, your joy, your peace, and your miracle mentality. You have the power to accelerate or decelerate your destiny.

There are 12 things that I do and have done for many years now that I believe wholeheartedly have accelerated my destiny. I like to call them **The Dynamic Destiny Dozen.** Each of these 12 principles and strategies has been utilized by 90% of people of greatness for hundreds of years. Allow me to caution you though. The Dynamic Destiny Dozen are not rocket science concepts. They are simple and not that difficult to implement as long as you have a willing heart, an open mind, and a productive spirit. In fact some of these principles you may already be utilizing, but perhaps more at the unconscious level. I challenge you to be intentional about implementing these concepts consciously, so that you can walk in the power of who you really are.

1. Discover and fulfill your purpose in life! The reality is this. Most people end up doing a good job at the wrong thing in life, in business, in relationships, and in finances because they never discovered the true purpose of these things. The people that live a life of true greatness and fulfillment know who they are, and why they are. They are crystal clear as to the assignment that their gifting solves in this world, and they dedicate their lives to doing what they love. Take the time to search your soul, inventory your gifts, talents,

and passions and get clarity in your life. **You see, the reason why discovering your purpose accelerates your destiny is because it produces CLARITY in your life.** Most people are not clear about what they want, who they want, why they want, and how they want. They go through life experimenting, testing and searching, rarely finding what they really do love and feel birthed to facilitate. They lead rather empty lives of quiet desperation.

But not you! Smiles. Not you my friend. You are a person of purpose and through this book and other empowerment materials you will apprehend or capture your destiny and success – the moment you get clear about it. Most people can tell you what they don't like faster than they can tell you what they like. They can tell you what job they don't want faster than they can describe their ideal dream career. **When you know the purpose of a thing, you become crystal clear about how to use it and maximize it.** Well, that being the case, in order to maximize your life and the lives of others around you, you've gotta get clear about your purpose.

> *"In order to be great, and live life over the top, you must stop being a wondering generality, and become a determined specific."*
> Zig Ziglar
>
> *"One half of knowing what you want is knowing what you must give up before you get it."*
> Sidney Howard

2. Commit to never being satisfied with your potential. Most people are just like icebergs, 70 – 90% of their greatness remains hidden below the waterline. Few people, great people, people like you – make the deliberate decision to invert their iceberg and **get most of their greatness OUT of them and into this world.** Potential is nothing more than the gap that exists between where you are and where you want to be. With that said, let me ask you a question. Do you have potential for more? **Do you have the potential to do more,** be more, achieve more, give more, love more, contribute more, celebrate more, reward more, smile more, earn

more, grow more, encourage more, save more, learn more, teach more, experience more, and just be more? Well if the answer is yes, then you, my friend, have amazing potential. Now, my challenge to you is to not be satisfied with that. **Close the gap on your greatness! Catch up...not to others, but to yourself!**

"Healthy dissatisfaction with your present is the birthplace for a great future!"
Dr. Mike Murdock

3. Create and seize destiny opportunities. My friend one of the key differences between those who master life and success versus those who don't is their ability to recognize, create, and maximize the opportunities that exist around them. The word opportunity is defined as "a set of circumstances creating a chance or possibility for advancement." Notice that the definition does not use the adjective "easy" in front of the word circumstances. Because truth be told, the old adage is sage advice indeed.

"The greatest opportunities in life are often disguised as hard work!"
Author Unknown

One of the most powerful things that you can do to get out of the "normal ninety" and into the "talented tenth" is to look for, proactively create, maximize, and then create for others this wonderful blessing in life called "opportunity." Why do millions of people line up for days and days to get on American Idol? Opportunity. Why do millions of people show up to interview for The Apprentice? Opportunity. Why do billions of people get up each morning and go to work? Opportunity. Why do millions of people each day, visit online dating websites? They are searching for the right relationship opportunity. Why do companies spend millions and even billions of dollars on advertising? Because they are proactively creating a set of circumstances that will give their company the opportunity to service your needs and wants. Why did you buy and are now reading this book? Because you made a quality decision to be *Fueled by Greatness* and seize an opportunity for growth and development. For more information about how to create and seize opportunities consider purchasing my book <u>Robbing the Grave of its Greatness.</u> In that book, I dedicate an entire chapter to this amazing concept, and it too will accelerate your destiny.

> *"Opportunity always takes NOW for an answer!"*
> Dr. John Maxwell
>
> *"Preparation is the greatest invitation to the right opportunities!"*
> Delatorro McNeal, II
>
> *"Don't just seek out opportunities for yourself, but also be the opportunity for others! Don't just look for open doors for yourself, but also be the open door for another!"*
> Delatorro McNeal, II

4. Embrace and celebrate the process of success. Most people don't like the process of getting from one place to another. Most people would prefer to just snap their fingers and go from rags to riches and miss the experience of learning how to manage their finances or understand how to systematically build and maintain wealth! Most would rather blink their eyes and go from single to happily married, and skip over the process of filtering through good relationships and bad ones. We live in a microwave society and an information age. This means that destiny is automatically sped up simply by the reality that access to information is more available now than ever before. You see, many people end up giving up, or turning back on the journey to greatness because they don't like the process. And many times, the reason they don't like the process is because they don't celebrate the process. **You see, I catch most people in**

life just groaning through, instead of growing through. They abort the final product (a wonderfully fulfilled life), because they didn't enjoy the process. We always hear people say, "Well the grass is greener on the other side!" But what we fail to remember is that there is also a lot more cow manure over there! **Success is not cheap, neither is fulfillment and contentment.** They each have a price attached to them, but the beautiful thing is that the reward is worth it my friend, it truly is worth it. Mediocrity, average living, and mundane existence carries a healthy price tag also. Everything has a price and the question is will you pay the price of the process to live a great life, or settle for second best? You deserve the best, so go after it!

"Stop fast-forwarding and rewinding your life, let it powerfully play out in your favor!"
Delatorro McNeal, II

5. Master and market your passion. We hear over and over again in motivational and self-help books to find your passion, right? Nowadays that phraseology and ideology is not new, **however what I do believe is rather new is the command to master that passion once you have found it.** It is one thing to find a passion, but if all you do is find it, you end up being a person with a lot of zeal but no fruit in life. You've gotta make the decision to discover your passion, and then get extremely good at it. **Tiger Woods would not be who he is and where he is if he just "found" golf.** No, no, no my friend. He found golf and it became his obsession. He mastered it! And once he mastered it, he with the help and mentorship of his father, marketed that which he had mastered, and now he wins major Golf Tournaments all over the world. So the question quickly becomes this. What is the one gift, talent, ability or skill that you are willing to master in life? Once you know that, the second question becomes who needs to know that you have mastered that gift once you have done so? Because it is not the most talented people in this world who get the most recognition, rather it's the ones who know how to put their gifts out into the marketplace that get the customers and the visibility! So my challenge to you, my friend, is three-fold. **First, don't just find your passion, discover and**

uncover it. It may take some work, soul searching, prayer, mediation, focused study, and research, but do whatever you have to in order to uncover it. **Second, polish that passion with expertise. Become an expert at your passion.** Get relentless with it. Take whatever positive steps you can to craft your passion. **Third, put your passion on display.** Market yourself and let the right types of people and groups know about your passion. And once the right people see you doing what you love, doing it amazingly well, and impacting lives with it, you will be light-years ahead of "the competition" and you will be fueled by the greatness of your passion and the greatness that you are igniting within others.

6. Write, word, and work your goals. First have a vision for your life, every area of your life. Decide today to be a person who commits things to paper. Dr. Mike Murdock says that a short pencil beats a long memory any day of the week! Some of the greatest inventions and business ideas began as urgent thoughts scribbled on small sheets of hotel room paper or hospital napkins. Get your vision out of your head and onto paper now! Write the vision, the goals, and the dreams that you have down so that you can see them. **The human mind loves imagery!** And we as humans typically pursue what we see, so if you see it, you will strive towards it. Once you have envisioned your goals and written them down, you must word them! That means you have to speak them. But be careful, only speak your goals to people that can help you achieve them!

I know many people who detoured their destiny not because they had a lack of passion towards their goals, and not because their goals were not written down, **but rather because they opened their mouths and told their most intimate and precious goals to toxic people** who did not believe in their dream. The weeds of negative words and expressions choked the life out of their dream. Don't allow that to happen to you. I only share my goals with a very small, select group of people who can hold me accountable and celebrate with me during the process and upon completion. You should do the same.

> *"The reason I am more successful than most is because I have failed more than most!"*
> Robert Kiyosaki

7. Overcome and capitalize on your pain. Pain is the greatest detour to greatness, period! I would venture to say that 95% of people don't get to their ultimate dream life in their careers, relationships, finances, and spiritual lives because they allowed the push of pain to force them to exit or U-turn way too early. In fact many people allow the pain in their lives to make them pull over on the side of the road of life and stall out, trying then to thumb a ride on the tailwind of the success of others! My friend, hear me well, the litmus test of whether or not you can handle this thing called greatness is your ability to overcome the painful experiences in life and then capitalize on them – hence using them to your advantage. Pain in life will cause you to either get better, or get bitter! One of the best books I have ever read on this subject is a book by one of my mentors Dr. John Maxwell. The name of the book is called **Failing Forward** and it tells the failure stories of some of the world's most successful people. That book changed my life in so many ways, because it taught me that **there is NO success without failure and pain.** Every story, every single one of them, had an element – and many times multiple elements of pain that compelled a person to get "inspirationally dissatisfied" enough with their situation to make a radical shift into a positive and productive direction. This shift created ultimate success for them, and it can do the same for you.

People often ask me in interviews as well as in coaching sessions how I have been able to accomplish so much in such a short amount of time, and I always tell them that I did not allow pain to keep me down. Think about it for a moment, what is the common element to the greatest books, movies, stories, articles, and shows that have transformed your life and thinking? I can guarantee that those books, movies, stories, articles, and shows had some element of pain in them that you could relate to. Thus, you felt where the person was coming from and going through, but you still hoped deep within yourself that they would overcome their painful circumstance and

triumph in the end. Right? Well, the same is true with you. **If you really want to skip some levels in the growth and development process, bounce back faster than other people do.** Don't take painful situations personally. Know that the pain in your life whether it be professional, personal, spiritual, emotional, or financial is trying to signal you that something is not right (i.e. your perspective, your expectations, your information, your level of connectedness, your attitude, your perception, your ideology, your paradigm, your level of dependency, your rationale, your habits, and so forth), and it is also trying to facilitate a better you in the process.

> *"Remember that a set back, is only a set up, for your comeback!"*
> Willie Jolley
>
> *"When you fall, simply land on your back; because if you can look up, you can get up!"*
> Les Brown

8. Master the power of mentorship. I love this subject because personally this strategy has brought me so much success. This principle accelerates your destiny so very much, but it costs so very much also. A mentor is defined as *a wise and trusted counselor or teacher.* The great thing about a mentor is that there is no age cap on mentors, no gender cap, no racial or cultural cap either. You can be mentored by someone younger than you, older than you, a different color than you, a different nationality than you. It really does not matter, because again based on the definition it is anyone whom you consider to give you wise and trusted counsel, advice, or instruction. Every person of greatness has someone in their lives that mentors and/or coaches them to greatness. Over the course of my life and career I can truly say that I would not be nearly as far as I am now – without the mentorship of a multitude of people. So, let me ask you. **Who are the mentors in your life right now?** Who are the people taking you to the next level on a regular basis? The individuals who have succeeded more than you and who you look up to for wisdom on how to get where they are?

_____

_____

_____

Congratulations. Good, now that you have told me who some of your mentors are, allow me to ask you another question. **How have these people mentored you? What did they do, say, or think that cut your learning curve or pushed you forward?** If you have ever been inspired by someone to do something great in your life, then my friend, you have been Fueled by Greatness! So go ahead, tell me what those mentors did in your life that inspired you.

_____

_____

_____

Okay, now I hope you have answers marked down for both of these activities because if you don't that means that you don't have mentors, and that is a problem. But guess what, not for long, because if you have never had a mentor, I would like to be your first! Now, I am not promising you personal coaching and all that stuff for free, but I am committing to do what I have done over the past few pages, which is to document my wisdom and ideas into formats that you can invest in to get you where you want to be. **You see, mentors don't have to be people who you have a personal or intimate relationship with,** but they can be people you admire, whose books you read, whose shows you watch, or whose principles you practice and success tips you emulate.

Now if you did list people and practices that were effective in mentoring you in life then you can attest to the fact that mentors do indeed help you accomplish more then you would have on your own. **I believe that we should always be on the lookout for people to mentor us.** Just as our goals and dreams and passions and ventures change and evolve – our mentors should grow and evolve as well.

You should have a mentor in any area of your life that you want to experience rapid success in. If you are a college student, you should have a mentor while you're in college who will help to guide you through college and into your dream career. If you are a business professional, you should have a mentor in your life who is helping you climb the corporate ladder and helping you get where you want to be. If you are in ministry, you should have someone who has succeeded at a much higher level than you have who will sharpen you and help you launch your vision. If you are an entrepreneur you need to connect with a mentor who has done the level of business that you aspire towards. Again, you need to find a mentor in any area of your life that you want rapid and consistent success in. Find someone who has been there and done that, and add them to your master mind team. So let me ask you, what areas of your life need a mentor? And how are you going to attract the mentor that you need into your life?

_____

_____

_____

Listen all mentorship relationships are gonna cost you either time, talent, treasure, or a combination of the three. For example, to be mentored by me in speaking and publishing like each of the dynamic co-authors of this book have been – they all had a pay a price. That price included money, their time, and I demanded the best of their speaking and writing talent to make this project a success. In this book, you are going to be mentored by each person through their chapter in their own unique way.

Mentorship works in both directions too. If you want to accelerate your destiny, mentor someone else. *"Well Del, how does mentoring someone else help me achieve success faster?"* Great question my friend. **Protégés force you to make sense out of your failures,** because they don't want to make the same mistakes that you did. They ask the types of questions that allow them to learn from your pain, without experiencing it themselves. So if you want to get over your issues faster, teach your life lessons to a protégé, and watch your "failure" turn into goldmine wisdom that will literally save their life!

It is a beautiful thing. And all the great people that I know use this tool to accelerate their greatness. **In summary, mentorship is the systematic investment into the people, paradigms, and principles that collapse time and empower rapid and sustained growth, development, contribution and destiny mastery!**

9. **Balance your life.** If you are more successful at work than you are at home, something is wrong with your life and you will never live the ultimate level of greatness that you were designed to. Why? Because somewhere along this journey of life you have been convinced and conditioned to invest 150% of yourself in the thing that brings you a paycheck, and your family/personal life get the leftovers! **Well, that ideology and psychology produces impotent interpersonal relationships and destroys good marriages and families.** My friend, please listen because I see millions of people each year that get this one all wrong. They think that the harder they work at their jobs the more they will be able to eventually please their families financially. And in the process of getting to the "there" in life they end up raping themselves, their families, their spouses, and their children of the quality time, dedication, and devotion that is so desperately needed. In today's society the TV and the internet raise our children, and we wonder why we have so many problems. **Let's go back to the basics! Balance your life.** Work as hard as you play, and play as hard as you work. Now if you are one who plays way too much and has not began to take life, success, and fulfillment seriously then get with the program. For every award you win at work, check to see if you are winning awards with your family and close friends. Awards of love, contentment, understanding, compassion, being there, and connectedness. Businesswoman, don't give all your energy to your job and then come home and not give any energy to your husband. That is jacked up! Businessman, don't give all your energy to your company, only to get home and neglect your children for a night out with the fellas! That is jacked up too!

Too much of anything can be bad for you, so you have to learn to balance things out. Infuse your days with balance! Try not to take your professional stress out on personal relationships, and simultaneously try not to allow personal issues (breakups, arguments, misunderstandings, and money problems) rob you of

performing your best within your company. **Be as diligent about scheduling vacations as you are about attending major conferences.** Schedule "me time" just as faithfully as you would a doctor's appointment and see how much more rewarding life will be for you. Celebrate every milestone and goal that you accomplish. Don't cash in personal happiness for professional accolade. If you implement what you learn in this book and many other great books, the reality is **YOU CAN HAVE IT ALL.** If you balance your life, you can be an award winning professional and an award winning parent, spouse, community member, and overall human being.

"My private measure of success is a daily question. If this were to be the last day of my life, would I be content with it? To live in a harmonious balance of commitments and pleasures is what I strive for."
Jane Rule

10. Better your best! Anthony Robbins, who has been named One of the Greatest Influencer's of our Generation, speaks often about the importance of a Japanese business philosophy called CANI!: Continual And Never-ending Improvement. Bill Gates continues to top himself as one of the wealthiest people in the world according for Forbes Magazine. James Brown, when asked in an interview which performance out of his hundreds-of-thousands was his best replied, "The one I will do tomorrow!" Over lunch one day with the world's greatest authority on leadership, Dr. John C. Maxwell, he told me one of the greatest disciplines that a person can commit to is that of being a lifelong learner! Each of these tremendously successful and significant people subscribe to a paradigm of greatness that I coined, "Better Your Best!" **Each morning a person of greatness wakes up, they try to do something small that day to top what they did the day before.** They commit to learning something new that day. They commit to meeting someone new that day. They commit to seeing a new beauty in life that day. They commit to being grateful in a new way that day. They commit to trying something new that day. They commit to competing only against themselves to see if they can top themselves and better their best, and many times they do just that! Dr. Steven Covey calls this the practice of Sharpening the Saw.

> *"The secret to your success or failure is hidden in your daily agenda!"*
> Dr. John Maxwell
>
> *"The rest of your life is the best of your life."*
> Dr. Dave Martin

My friend, you have the ability to take a daily inventory of what works and what doesn't work in your life, your family, your finances, your emotions, your plans, your goals, your attitudes, and your situations. Be a person who knows when to shed your skin and show forth a new coat of excellence. **Know when things are getting stale, routine, dull, and boring – then make a commitment to bring about a freshness each day in that area.** Read one book per month, rather than one book per year. Millionaires do. Watch one to two hours of television per day, rather than EIGHT HOURS of television per day. Why? Because input determines output, and if you put low quality things into your mind, you will get low quality things out. Similarly, if you invest in the great things going in, of course great things will come back out. **Today counts!** Use it to top yourself. Be a better husband tomorrow than you were today. Be a sexier wife tomorrow than you were today. Be a more loving parent tomorrow than you were today. Be a more integrity-focused businessperson today then you were yesterday. **Realize that your best is still inside you, use the TODAY of everyday to get your best out, and when you've done your best, wake up tomorrow and better it!**

> *"Whatever you do today, do it better tomorrow!"*
> Robert Schuller

> *"Empty the coins of your purse into your mind and your mind will fill your purse with coins."*
> Benjamin Franklin

> *"I remind myself every morning: Nothing I say this day will teach me anything. So if I'm going to learn, I must do it by listening."*
> Larry King

11. Develop a winning personality. I will never forget the day that I met George Ross from the NBC hit television show *The Apprentice.* George Ross has been Donald Trump's Real Estate Attorney for more than twenty years! I met him at a Millionaire's Conference in Tampa in January of 2006. I had the unique privilege and opportunity to spend 30 to 45 minutes in his presence and while speaking with him I asked him to tell me the top strategy for success that he has used, that has made him successful. Now, you have to understand something, this guy has done over 700 different real estate transactions for The Donald, and has been a close advisor to Donald Trump for many years so I was expecting some really grand terminology and some big complicated concept. But I was shockingly surprised when he smiled at me, put his hand on my shoulder, gave me a gentle squeeze and said, *"Son you are gonna go very far in life, and you will be very successful in business!"* I smiled really big, and asked him why he felt that way. He continued to say, *"Because you ask awesome questions that empower you to inspire others, and that is a great trait that you have, and I picked up on it right away!"* Well, thank you so very much I replied. Then he continued to tell me the first of three great principles that he uses to guide his life and success. **He told me that the number #1 thing that a person should have in order to be great is a Winning Personality!** He said, *"Delatorro if people like you, they will do business with you. If they like you they will buy from you, sell to you, negotiate with you, partner with you, get behind your vision, support your dreams, and so forth."* I could not agree more with George Ross.

I have met great success not because I am the smartest person, or the wealthiest person, or the most handsome, but one thing that God blessed me with is a **Winning Personality,** and my friend, that alone has opened doors for me that wealth, looks, and intelligence simply could not. Pay attention to the two words George used. He did not say that you have to have just a personality, because we all possess that, and many people in fact have a very negative one right? Smiles. But he mentions a very specific type of personality that we can adopt and display that can literally change the world.

He challenges us all to have a "winning" personality. To me that means that we must possess a personality that **completes rather than competes.** One that **celebrates not complicates.** One that **builds bridges, rather than brick walls.** One that says the totality of the whole is greater than the sum of its parts. People who possess a winning attitude empower others to win as well. In business, they don't just want all the success for themselves, but rather they want to share the success on both sides of the transaction. Families with winning personalities function like a team. They love each other, support each other, pray for each other, and invest in each other's passions. Make a fresh commitment today to be a person that consistently displays a contagiously winning personality and watch how much faster you get to that place called "there" in your life.

> *"Success is not a see-saw. Others don't have to go down, just so that you can go up. Rather success is like an elevator, we can all go up together!"*
> Delatorro L. McNeal, II
>
> *"Attitude is everything!"*
> Keith Harrell
>
> *"You can't hold another person down, without staying down with them!"*
> Booker T. Washington

12. Never give up. This one will be very short because it is self explanatory! Listen friend, the highway to greatness and your destiny is paved with painful experiences and failure. **But it's really not about what happens to you, it is what you do about it, and how you react to it that determines your world.** No person of excellence got to where they are by throwing in the towel. Make a commitment to be like a stamp, and stick to one thing until it delivers! If you know the race is 5 miles long, and you have the intention of quitting 3 miles into it, you might as well not even start the race. **The purpose of the race is NOT to see who can start, anyone can do that, the true purpose and prize of a race is to see who can finish!** In order to finish you must develop the fortitude to not give up when things get hard, which they will. If you know people in your life right now who are quitters, STOP INVESTING TIME in them immediately! All they will do is condition you towards quitting things in your life.

Later in this book, you will learn that sometimes It's Okay to Quit, but I will let Omicron Long explain that concept to you. It is cutting edge, and you will be blessed by it. Finishers hang around finishers. Winners spend time with winners. Destiny people associate with destiny people. Visionaries enjoy the company of other visionaries. To make sure that you don't give up, associate with people that don't give up. My mentors won't let me quit, although I have wanted to at times. Because of the right relationships in my life, those negative ideas only went as far as fleeting thoughts, and never into executed actions. I want you to participate in an activity with me right now. I am going to start a sentence and I want you to finish it for me. Yes, I want you to write your answers below.

1. No matter how hard life gets,

_____ *I will never give up* _____! (*this is your answer*)

2. No matter how lonely this journey gets,

_____!

3. No matter how financially strapped I get,

_____!

4. No matter how intimidating the competition may seem,

_____!

5. No matter if others don't believe in my dream,

_____!

6. No matter if my family does not support me,

_____!

7. No matter the obstacle, my dream reminds me that

_____!

> *"Never quit because you are giving up, only quit because you are going up!"*
> Willie Jolley
>
> *"Never, ever, ever...give up!"*
> Sir Winston Churchill

Chapter Summary

- ☐ Discover your purpose early in life
- ☐ Commit to never being satisfied with your potential
- ☐ Create and seize destiny opportunities
- ☐ Embrace and celebrate the process of success
- ☐ Master and market your passion
- ☐ Write, word, and work your goals
- ☐ Overcome and capitalize on your pain
- ☐ Master the power of mentorship
- ☐ Balance your life
- ☐ Better your best
- ☐ Develop a winning personality
- ☐ Never give up

Prepare to be Fueled by the Wisdom of
Dawn Pici

America's leading authority on *Starting Over,* **Dawn Pici** is an award winning **Speaker, Author,** and **Success Coach** who has impacted audiences worldwide, inspiring them to expand the dimensions of their professional and personal lives. As CEO and founder of *Your Step Beyond,* a company that empowers people to re-start their lives and careers, Dawn has had a 15 year career of delivering high **energy, experiential** and **informative** messages to stimulate human potential. Drawing from years of teaching experience and 20 years of success in sales and marketing, Dawn addresses a wide range of audiences from **business, education,** and **faith based** organizations.

Internationally known for her *"Turning Points"* keynote presentation, she has empowered audiences to redefine and redesign their lives and careers. Dawn's marketing and motivational secrets give business people an **unbeatable edge** in gaining, retaining and cultivating a strong customer base.

Her fast paced, entertaining programs will increase performance, create focus, and rekindle hope for reaching ones true potential and destiny. **POWERFUL** and **PURPOSEFUL,** Dawn desires for YOU to take **Your Step Beyond** and lay hold of **your dreams!**

Website: www.YourStepBeyond.com
Email: Dawn@YourStepBeyond.com

GRAB YOUR GREATNESS!

> *"The only true measure of success is the ratio between what we might have done and what we might have been on one hand, and the thing we have made and the thing we have have made of ourselves on the other."*
> H.G. Wells

Regardless of your age, occupation, personal or financial situation, you are DESTINED for GREATNESS!

Sounds crazy doesn't it? I don't even know you or your situation. How can I make such a claim? The fact that you are reading this book indicates that you are **LOOKING** for something. Perhaps you are saying, "I want more out of my life," or "I wish I could start over." The most beautiful and inspiring aspect of human life is that every day we have the opportunity to **STEP BEYOND** our current level of existence and **GRAB** the **GREATNESS** planted inside each and **EVERYONE** of us!

GREATNESS IS inside of YOU and the rest of us **NEED YOU!** We need to be touched by the unique brand of greatness only **YOU** possess. There are innovations and ideas that only **YOU** will discover that will improve our lives, businesses, schools, communities, and churches. These discoveries will only be revealed when **YOU** commit to your dreams and goals. **YOU** are like my new computer, full of programs and ready to go. **YOU** are loaded with potential, but profit no one by just sitting on the desk, unused, day after day. **YOU** need someone skilled to unlock all that is within.

> *"If you could get up the courage to begin,*
> *you have the courage to succeed."*
> David Viscott

There is no time to waste. You've got places to go, lives to touch and new horizons to experience. I'm going to get you going with **Three Dynamic "D's"** that will begin your journey and reveal the greatness inside of you.

DESIRE

Imagine typing an important document on your computer all day long, only to realize that you forgot to turn the computer on. **Desire** is the element that "turns on" our ability to **seek** the greatness inside. Desire is the catalyst which propels us to the next level. It gives us the courage to move forward. Your desire caused you to pick up this book. There is something you want that has eluded you.

WHAT IS IT?

I want the **FIRST** thing that pops into your head. **WHY** are you reading this book? **WHAT** are you looking to change? Improve upon? Get rid of? Do differently? Add to your life? Are you looking to advance at work or find a new job altogether? Have you always dreamed of starting your own business or do you want to change careers? Perhaps you are looking for personal development. Do you want to improve your attitude or your relationships with others. Do you feel as though you've been spinning your wheels? Working hard but getting nowhere? Some of you might be thinking that you want to change EVERYTHING. You simply want to start over.

What would make you happy, contented and fulfilled?
Write it down in the box below.

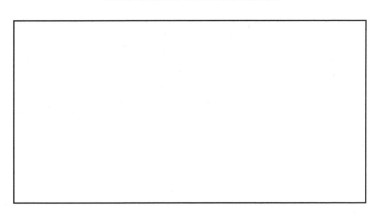

Go on. Get a pencil or pen and write it down.
Don't you dare go a step further until you get this on paper.

I sound like your mother, don't I? Please realize I want you to get the MOST out of this book. We need to get your computer turned on if you're going to get anywhere. So get up and go find something to write with. I'll wait….. (Small joke).

Now that you have identified your **DESIRE** you are ready for step two:

DECISION

 "Decide and then… stop deciding!" Dawn Pici

One of the finest aspects of my computer is that once I select a program to work in, the computer does not change its mind and

suddenly switch to another. It will continue to work in the program I have selected until I am finished. One day I realized I needed to be more like my computer. I needed to

MAKE a DECISION and then MAKE it WORK.

All too often people make decisions, but when the going gets tough or they are forced out of their comfort zone, they **decide** to do something else. They decide to do this, and then they decide to do that. They never stop deciding. Cortez had an answer for this. His men had a fierce battle before them. There was a choice. They could fight or return home in their ships. He burned the boats so that his men would have no option for retreat. This made his men fight harder and win the battle. Make a decision to go after your desire, and then…

STOP DECIDING.

What decision do you need to make in order to achieve your hearts desire? For instance, let's say you would like to go into business for yourself. Perhaps the decision you need to make involves pursuing information regarding that field. Maybe you are looking to change careers. If so, you might make a decision to be re-trained. What if your desire is for self- improvement? Availing yourself to motivational books and CD's would be helpful.

Review your desire and write in the space below a decision you will make to aid you in accomplishing it.

A **DESIRE** without a **DECISION** is like a computer without a hard drive. It will produce **NOTHING** and get you **NO WHERE**. And **YOU** are going places! So put that decision in writing **NOW!**

Many people stop here because they are afraid to make a decision. They are afraid to make a mistake, afraid to commit, afraid of failure or success. My husband has great advice for this. He reminds folks that, "A decision NOT made is, nonetheless, a decision made. "You will either make a decision to run after your desire and *Grab Your Greatness,* or you will side step that decision and essentially 'decide' to remain as you were the day you picked up this book.

DETERMINATION

> *Character is the ability to carry out a worthwhile decision, after the emotion of making that decision has passed."* Dennis Waitley

I have been a motivational speaker for many years. In that time I have seen thousands upon thousands of well meaning people make decisions regarding self improvement of some sort. They make these decisions with a great deal of emotion and sincerity. Some write these decisions down and even make public professions declaring their determination to achieve the goal they have chosen. Despite all of this hoopla, very small percentages actually follow through and persevere to achieve their dreams.

WHAT WENT WRONG?

The American Heritage Dictionary defines **determination** as, "a fixed movement or tendency toward some object or end." Pay particular attention to the words.

FIXED MOVEMENT ... TOWARD.

Decisions alone achieve NOTHING. What you are looking for is a TURNING POINT. A turning point is a place in your life where you make a decision and then apply **fixed movement toward** your goal. Decisions alone create frustration and embarrassment. Decisions powered by movement or action toward your goal will propel you to achieve your goals and will build your self-esteem.

Moving toward your goal will also launch you into new and exciting areas you may not have foreseen. A perfect example is this book. I met several of the authors of this book at a conference for motivational speakers. We share a **desire** for self improvement in our field. Each of us made a **decision** to move toward that goal by attending conferences and seminars. Our **determination** caused us to follow through and attend one particular conference. At that conference, in addition to the excellent training each of us received, we began to visualize *Fueled By Greatness.* Our **desire** for this book project caused us to make a **decision** to create it. **Determination** caused us to give up time and energy to produce our individual chapters. You are now receiving the benefit of our **desire, decision and determination.** We are receiving the satisfaction and self esteem that comes from goal achievement.

Did you notice that writing this particular book was not part of our original desire? This is one of the marvelous benefits you will receive by employing determination to your decisions. As you move toward your desire other doors will open that you could never have imagined.

Do **YOU** want to be part of the 20% of visionaries who not only make decisions but turn them into reality? If so, you need to be aware of the **enemies** of determination. Just like the viruses that attack and destroy the programs in my computer, these enemies can keep you from **Grabbing the Greatness** inside of you. Beware!

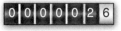

They are:
- **Present DOUBTS**
- **Past DEFEATS**

Present DOUBTS

Present doubt is the KILLER of desire. Doubt strangles every talent; stirs every negative emotion; stops every attempt at forward motion. Doubt gets its energy from FEAR. Many times, doubt is rooted in past defeats.

Past DEFEATS

Past defeats come in two varieties, hurt and disappointment. Hurt and disappointment can be placed on us from other people or situations beyond our control. They can also result from the pain we have brought on ourselves from poor choices.

You have past defeats and present doubts that are currently holding you back from believing you can have the desire your heart is aching for. How do I know this? Because you are human and if you didn't have them it wouldn't be fair to the rest of us who are struggling. I want you to write down one doubt and one defeat that you are willing to conquer.

Present Doubt

Past Defeat

> *"Your past is important, but it is not important enough to control your future."*
> Zig Ziglar

THE CURE

Whether you are dealing with one or a combination of both of these enemies, there is hope for YOU. When a computer picks up a virus, there are certain procedures we must follow to get it functioning properly again.

First, we clean up the hard drive. We erase certain files that have been corrupted. Second, we install new software. Third, we renew our anti-virus protection.

Unlike computers, it is not always desirable to 'erase' the entire negative that has been put into our lives. To do so would also erase all that we have LEARNED from those experiences. However, we do need to erase the negative energy these unhappy experiences have left behind. Negative energy produces negative thoughts. Negative thoughts generate the doubt and fear to move forward, thwarting determination. Negative thoughts will destroy our present and future in the same way that viruses 'eat up' all of our valuable files.

To 'clean up' our hard drive and empower ourselves to function effectively, we install new software. That software comes in the form of positive affirmations, motivational material and associations with encouraging people who will hold us accountable for our actions. My computer works on the principle of 'garbage in – garbage out.' The same is true with humans. If we want to change the amount of garbage going out of our lives and decisions, we will need to change what is going in.

Finally, we install and update our anti-virus protection. Anti-virus protection for humans can be summed up in one word: **FOCUS.**

> *"Life can be understood backwards,*
> *but it must be lived forwards."*
> John L. Mason

PLACE YOUR FOCUS ON YOUR FUTURE

Everyday effort must be spent on planning, practicing and providing for your wonderful future. Remember the words **FIXED MOVEMENT TOWARD?   Movement** implies action. **YOU** are **DOING** something related to the desired goal. Action will conquer doubt and fear every time.

Fixed movement refers to movement that is **CONSISTENT.** Like a runner on the home stretch pressing hard toward the finish line, we must **powerfully persist** if we are to **Grab** our **Greatness.**

> *"Winning is not a sometime thing. It's an all*
> *the time thing. Winning is a habit."*
> Vince Lombardi

Finally, we need to apply this effort in the correct direction. We must press **TOWARD** our goal. Looking back and re-living hurts and failures will destine us to re-create these in our present and future. That's not for **YOU! YOU** are moving on from where you are today. **YOU** have what it takes to accomplish your dreams!

> *"The most important three words*
> *you can say to yourself:*
> *YES I CAN!"*
> Dennis Waitley

I entitled this chapter Grab your Greatness because GRABBING for anything requires desire, decisiveness and determination. As you put these elements together you WILL achieve your dreams! Resist your self-doubt and persist until YOUR desire is YOUR reality!

YOU are destined for GREATNESS because GREATNESS is inside of YOU!

<u>Chapter Summary</u>

- ☐ Regardless of your current situation, you are DESTINED for GREATNESS!
- ☐ We NEED your greatness to be manifested in our world!
- ☐ Decide to pursue your desire--- then STOP deciding!
- ☐ Develop the determination to MAKE IT WORK!
- ☐ FOCUS on your FUTURE – not past defeats or present doubts.
- ☐ Repeat after me –YES I CAN!

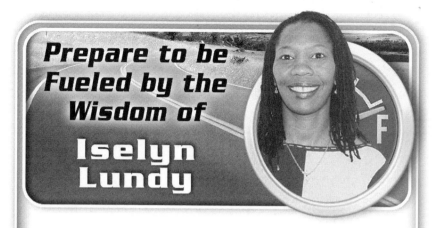

Iselyn Hamilton-Lundy is known to teenage audiences as "the cool mom" and is affectionately known as "Diva Lundy" to her friends. She is a Certified Family Nurse Practitioner who specializes in infant and adolescent medicine. She received her Bachelor's and Master's degrees from The University of South Florida. Iselyn is a powerful voice in the speaking industry because of her unique ability to relate to teens on their level without being "too preachy" and still get the message across. She has wowed audiences with her presentations at church functions, juvenile detention centers, hospitals and seminars. The energy she possesses is evident in her daily work with adolescents, as well as the keynote addresses she presents. Her talents are uniquely displayed in her book, *"Don't Let Your Elevator Get Stuck on Stupid: Survival Tips for Teens."* She uses a combination of humor and seriousness help motivate teens from the ground floor of their life to the top floor so they can reach their next level of success.

Iselyn lives in Brandon, Florida with her two children. Her hobbies include traveling, listening to jazz music and spending time with family and friends.

Website: www.DucklingToDiva.com
Email: ilundy@tampabay.rr.com

GREATNESS IS A CHOICE

Have you ever waited for an elevator for what seemed like an eternity, and when you got on realized it was going in the wrong direction?

Have you ever gotten on an elevator and pressed the up button, but the elevator took you down instead?

Have you ever gotten on an elevator and pushed a destination but discovered that the elevator wasn't moving and you were stuck?

Have you ever wished you had the key to the penthouse where the opportunities were abundant?

Well, my friend, life is like an elevator. Think about it! An elevator starts at the ground floor and when you get on you have to make a decision to go up or down. Life starts you out on the ground level and you are faced with choosing what direction you want your life to move in.

An elevator is a simple concept; it is a compartment that has a lifting system attached to it. There are two choices of elevator lifting systems. A roped system, which is a simple rope that moves the elevator up or down with no motorized components. For easy comparison it is similar to tying a piece of rope to a box. The other is the hydraulic system, which consists of a tank that has a fluid reservoir (oil), and a pump that is powered by an electric motor. In order for the hydraulic elevator to move, the pump forces the fluid from the tank to a cylinder that causes the elevator to move up or down. **Before the elevator can move the fuel tank has to be filled.**

Both types will get the elevator to the top but the roped method uses a lot less energy and elevates slower. So let me ask you this: What systems or "pumps" do you have in place in your life to help you to elevate yourself to greatness? What choices have you made to put a "pump" in place to elevate your status? Are you afraid to use the fueled elevator that will elevate you faster? Have you settled for the slower choice? Are you stuck between the floors of the desire to want more and the fear of how to get there? Is your fuel tank full or empty? Most importantly have you made the choice to get on the elevator, fill up your fuel tank and push the buttons to elevate yourself to greatness? If so, I want you to commend yourself and continue reading because **I am going to help you help yourself make the choice for greatness.** Then I am going to tell you how to achieve greatness once the choice is made.

Envision yourself standing at a bank of elevators. Think about what it is you see. There is a door that opens and closes. The outside of the elevator has two buttons to choose from to go up or down. The top of the elevator doors has numbers on it that indicate the highest level the elevator will go. The inside of the elevator is made of three walls that enclose the compartment. There is a panel with the floor numbers, an emergency button and an emergency telephone. There is also an inspection certificate that lets you know the last time the elevator was inspected. Now that you have a clear picture of the elevator and I have established the components that make it up, I want to explain the purpose of an elevator so you can make a clear choice of where you will be going once you get on.

The purpose of an elevator is to help you to reach your destination faster. Taking the stairs will get you there but the elevator will get you there faster. Again this brings us back to choices. Do you choose to reach your greatness now or are you okay with the slower route? For example, are you someone who would fly to a destination because you will get there faster? Or are you someone who doesn't care when you get there as long as you do?

Are you the type of individual who will take the highway versus the service road because it is quicker and there are no traffic lights? If you have made the choice for the quicker elevation to greatness and want to cut your learning curve drastically this chapter is for you.

My friend, remember that although taking the elevator is faster, there may be times when a power outage may hit and you will be forced to take the stairs. During the times in your life when you are experiencing power outages, remember that **in order to continue your acceleration to the top you have to be willing to take the stairs; willing to drive instead of fly; and willing to take the service road instead of the highway.**

> *"I am going to help you help yourself make the choice for greatness."*

The inside of the elevator is equipped with an emergency telephone and emergency button. How many times have you suffered with a problem in your life alone and never reached out for help? How many times have you ignored phone calls from friends when you were "depressed" or having personal problems, and instead of reaching out to someone and talking about it, you stayed locked up in your room? Times like those are why there are emergency devices. You need to learn how to make the choice to push the emergency button to stop the elevator and pick up the phone to ask someone for help. Don't be afraid to sound the alarm. Don't waste the tools you are given. Use them for their intended purpose, which is to elevate you from your present situation.

It can be a stressful situation being stuck between floors in an elevator. For example, are you stuck between the second floor of "being separated" and the third floor of "divorce"? "Do you sit at home in despair because you are no longer attached to another individual? Have you ever considered that the reason you are where you are may be because you are not a separate individual in your own right? Instead of feeling sorry about the current status of your dating life, get out and celebrate who you are! No one is looking for a mopey mate and if you are feeling sorry for yourself you are moping. Instead of looking at this as a bad thing, think of it as your opportunity to meet the perfect mate for you because that person is out there just waiting for you to come along. Take this time to be ready when he or she does show up.

Open the door from separation to emancipation and allow for a new you to emerge. In 2004, I attended Delatorro McNeal's first motivational speaking boot camp. I received enough tools to not only get started, but to reach my desired goal in half the time it would have normally taken. Due to dealing with life issues such as divorce and family affairs, I am just now, two years later, pursuing and reaching my greatness goal. **Life is going to give you some stop signs along the way, when it does I want you to remember that the sign says stop, it doesn't say stay.** So fix the life issues and get back on your elevator climb to greatness because it is meant to be.

Consider the purpose of the inspection certificate. It is there to let the elevator passengers know that the elevator has been inspected and meets all safety requirements. Have you inspected the quality of your life? Does it meet your expectations? Does your introspection meet the quality of your inspection? If not, now is the time for a new inspection and an update on how to improve and elevate your standing in life.

Now that you understand the purpose of the elevator, let's discuss the concept of choices. The fact that you are standing at the elevator

means you have made a choice to be there. You chose to read this book today. The question to ask yourself is, Was it a clear choice? The ability to make a choice affords you the right, the power, and the chance to choose your destination and route of elevation. It also affords you the opportunity to make an alternate choice, or no choice at all, which is still a choice.

Remember that the choices you make will have an impact on how long it will take you to reach your level of greatness, or if you will reach it at all. Your choice may speed up or slow down your arrival time, or keep you stuck. So when making a choice keep in mind your ultimate goal: elevating yourself to greatness. Everyday we make choices about many aspects of our lives such as:

- Friends
- Finances
- Career
- Family
- Relationships
- Religion
- Traveling
- Health
- Lifestyle
- Transportation

The key to making choices that elevate you to greatness is knowing what the motivation is behind the choice. The root word of motivation is motive, which means inner drive; to incite or impel (push, drive, or move forward). What will it take to motivate you? **Most importantly who or what will you allow to motivate you?** For example, if you are motivated to lose weight, eat healthy and exercise, partnering with someone who hates exercise but loves to eat may not make for a great partnership. If you are motivated to stop smoking, making yourself accountable to someone who smokes is not a good choice. If you are motivated to become debt

Greatness is a Choice — *Iselyn Lundy*

free, getting advice from someone who lives paycheck to paycheck and visits advance paycheck companies on a regular basis is not a wise choice. If you are having relationship problems you might not want to get advice from someone who has been married four times and is working on spouse number five.

If you know you can afford the payment on a Toyota Corolla but buy a BMW instead, was the motivation for buying the BMW that you want people to see what you drive as opposed to letting them see what it is that's driving you? Do you go to work everyday to a job you hate, yet you have not allowed the person at the top of the success ladder to be the motivator you need to excel yourself into another position? If you answered yes to any of these questions, I am challenging you to examine what mindset you adopted to allow yourself not to be motivated to pursue greatness.

Mindset is a fixed mental attitude formed by things like experience, education, prejudice, or just getting through the stuff in life. **A person's mindset can either propel them to greatness or hinder them from reaching greatness. Keep in mind that a person's mindset can affect you directly or indirectly.**

In 1955, Rosa Parks sat on a city bus tired from a hard day's work and refused to give up her seat to a white man. Rosa decided that her elevator was full and she wasn't taking on any more passengers. Her mindset that day was the beginning of a boycott that affected an entire nation. Martin Luther King, Jr.'s mindset was one of equality by a means of nonviolence. Ironically, his death was at the hands of violence, but his death did not stop his movement, it propelled it to phenomenal heights. The positive effects of his vision are still being felt today.

Both incidents are examples of how **true greatness cannot be stopped, and how one person's mindset can have an indirect effect on countless people.** I'm sure Rosa nor Martin could have predicted how far reaching their efforts would be. So when you choose someone to mentor or motivate you, be certain that their mindset is parallel to yours so that you don't end up on an elevator ride that doesn't propel your goals.

Let's take a moment here before moving on to reflect and recap. So far we have discussed:

- Choosing a direction to greatness
- The purpose of elevating yourself to greatness
- Tools available to you on your journey to greatness
- Knowing when to sound the alarm
- Being willing to take an alternate route to success when "power outages" occur in life
- Choosing an appropriate motivator mindsets

WOW! All that and we still have to get on the elevator.

Here is where we will talk about how and why you will choose which elevator to get on, and which direction you want to go. Will you choose the first one that shows up because you think if you don't it may be a missed opportunity? Will you wait for the next one to see who is on it? Will you choose the one closest to you because it is simply that, closer? Will you choose the one that is crowded because you are the type of person who follows the crowd, and is content listening to someone else's elevator music?

Hillary Clinton was a good first lady but today she is a great senator, because she chose not to ride on her husband's elevator and be content with his elevator music; she chose her own direction and her own music, both were choices that propelled her to the top. Will you choose an elevator that is moderately crowded because it affords you an equal opportunity of choices? Will you wait for an empty elevator so you will be the only passenger because you like to lead the way without sharing your success? Whatever you choose make it a clear choice for greatness. **Make sure that with every door that opens and** every floor you get off on you strive for reaching your best potential. You will always have obstacles, but don't let them stop you. Obstacles that will slow down your acceleration:

- Not making a choice
- Letting other people make a choice for you
- Making the wrong choice
- Choosing to take the longer, slower route
- Not recognizing that you need to make a choice

In this chapter you have been informed, equipped and motivated to make the choice for greatness, so **I challenge you now to choose greatness.** If it takes an elevator two minutes to go from the ground floor to the second floor, I want you to now take two minutes to choose greatness as a destination for yourself.

THE CHOICE IS YOURS

Because I am a living testimony, I want you to take a moment now to email me at **ilundy@tampabay.rr.com** and give me your testimony on how you were encouraged to elevate yourself and succeed.

Chapter Summary

☐ First, make a choice for greatness; then
☐ Choose to reach greatness through elevation; then
☐ Be willing to take the stairs, drive instead of fly, or take the service lane instead of the highway when lifes power outages occur; then
☐ Use the tools you have to help elevate yourself on your journey to greatness; then
☐ Celebrate the rewards of your success!

Prepare to be Fueled by the Wisdom of Natasha Brown

Natasha Brown is an **Attorney, Professional Motivational Speaker, Author** and **Entrepreneur.** She is the founder, CEO, and President of *Designed for Destiny, Inc.*, a company based in Atlanta, Georgia, that is dedicated to inspiring, encouraging and equipping all people to fulfill their destinies.

As an **international speaker** and former **radio talk-show host**, Natasha has engaged her audiences with her unique presentation style. She has spoken for civic organizations, student groups, and churches encouraging her listeners to find their deeply hidden talents, the strength to succeed, and recognize their unique gifts to fulfill a specific purpose in life. Her messages inspire her audience to accept that they are each a one of a kind, specially created masterpiece – *"A DESIGNER ORIGINAL."*

Born and raised in Freeport, Bahamas, Natasha relocated to Atlanta to attend Clark Atlanta University. She graduated **magna cum laude** and earned her Bachelor of Arts Degree in Mass Media Arts. She received her **Juris Doctor** from John Marshall Law School-Atlanta.

Website: www.DesignedForDestiny.com
Email: Natasha@DesignedForDestiny.com

A DESIGNER ORIGINAL

> *"Every achiever that I have ever met says, 'My life turned around at the moment when I began to believe in me.'"*
> Dr. Robert H. Schuller

She stared at me from across the table in total amazement. Was she looking at a ghost? Her eyes were full of confusion. She shook her head in disbelief. After all, she thought she really knew me!

Here I was, an attorney with a good job in corporate America. I had a successful boyfriend, owned my own home, was involved in professional organizations, and very active in my church. She could not believe that I, of all people, was admitting that I had low self esteem.

For me, it started at an early age. The oldest of three girls, I have two beautiful sisters of whom I am very proud. My struggle with self esteem began because as a child I thought I had to compete with my sisters to get attention. "Nika is so pretty" and "Mandy is so cute," people would say. Maybe they said those things to me too, but I don't remember hearing it. I dwelled on my imperfections. So, how could I compete with two pretty, cute younger sisters?

Well, I found a way to get attention. I became a perfectionist. Seeking praise, I made good grades in school. I tried to stay out of trouble and be a "good girl." You may ask, did my mother say or do things that made me feel as if I were not as important as my sisters?

On the contrary, she always made each of us feel very special. My low self esteem developed out of my own negative thoughts and beliefs about myself. There was no one person or situation that created it. I didn't feel important, so I did what I had to do to get attention.

That day, my friend was seeing the real me for the first time. That was the day I dared to step out in the shoes crafted just for me. It was the day I showed the world the real me – my true self. It was the day I realized that I was someone special, wearing my very own custom designed shoes.
That day I accepted that I was *"A Designer Original."*
That day I accepted that I was *"Designed for Destiny."*

It was hard for my friend to believe that I suffered from low self esteem. She always looked at me as someone who had it all together. She even looked to me for inspiration when she was facing difficulties of her own. But low self esteem was a battle I fought for many years. It gripped me and kept me deep in depression. In the middle of it all, I functioned well. To cover up what I was really feeling, I wore stylish (but uncomfortable) shoes. No one knew, but I did. Although I was "functioning," I was missing something.

I was unable to walk in the **purpose** for which I was designed. Low self-esteem is one of the biggest reasons people live **without** purpose or worse yet, die with **unfulfilled** purpose. I don't want you to be in those same painful shoes. I want you to reach for your purpose and to achieve the **greatness** that lives inside **you**.

Are you where I was? Do you have the career? Do you look good and smell good? Yet, do you feel inferior? Do you wear a smile to cover up the pain? If you answered yes, then you're just like I was, wearing stylish, but wrong, shoes everyday and pretending to be someone you're not. But, how did you get there?

Right now, I want you to tell me who or what influenced your thoughts and beliefs about yourself.

_____

_____

_____

_____

If we are to fulfill our purpose and have our **greatness** exposed, we must believe in ourselves and forget about all the negative things everyone else ever said about us! We must step out in the shoes that have been made to fit us perfectly. I know it's hard…but that's why I'm here…to help. I want to **fuel** you for **greatness!**

> *"There are three things that are extremely hard: steel, a diamond, and to know one's self."*
> Ben Franklin

I will show you how to build your self-esteem. It's not easy, but just like finding that perfect pair of shoes, it's worth the work!

What is good self-esteem? How do you know if you have low self-esteem? First, self-esteem is how you see yourself. Many times, how we see ourselves is born out of what we've been told by others, thoughts we have in our own minds, and attitudes that have been passed down to us from our parents, or other significant people in our lives.

Good self-esteem requires that you have positive thoughts or attitudes about yourself. Good self-esteem allows you to see yourself as someone who is perfectly and wonderfully created. Good self-esteem allows you to say, "I am worthy." Good self esteem **propels** you into your purpose, because you accept that *you* have been created to complete a specific task on this earth.

Before we go any further, I want you to take a moment, and write down what you believe is good self-esteem.

_____

_____

_____

_____

Next, write what you *really* feel about yourself. Be truthful. Remember, in order to overcome a problem, you must be able to face it. Let's take a moment and do it right now. Go ahead, you have five minutes – I'm timing you. BEGIN!

THINGS I LIKE ABOUT ME:

THINGS I DON'T LIKE ABOUT ME:

_____   _____

_____   _____

_____   _____

_____   _____

_____   _____

Ok, TIME IS UP!

Was that a hard exercise for you? Yes or no? Why or why not?

_____

_____

_____

_____

Was it difficult for you to face yourself? Yes or no? Why or why not?

_____

_____

_____

_____

I know it isn't easy; I've been where you are. When you suffer from a lack of self-esteem, you don't know how you can ever feel good about yourself. However, there is hope, and I'm living proof that you can overcome your fears, begin to believe in yourself, and walk in the purpose for which you have been designed.

Developing good self-esteem is like wearing the perfect pair of shoes. They fit just right, they look good, and they're comfortable. You, my friend, are going to be *Fueled by Greatness,* just by learning how to shop for that perfect pair of shoes and build your self-esteem.

FIRST, YOU MUST FIND SHOES IN THE RIGHT STYLE

We all want shoes that look good, and just like wanting shoes that look good, we need to have the right beliefs about ourselves. There is no one else like you. The mold was broken the day you were born. You may have a hard time believing that there is anything special about you, but don't be mistaken! You are a one of a kind design.

You are special; you are a wonderfully created masterpiece. Never feel that there is anyone who is greater than you are. It does not matter where you were born, who your parents are, or the way you look. You have been perfectly designed to fulfill the purpose for which you are called to complete. Don't ever compare yourself to anyone else. No one else has a smile like yours that can brighten up a room; no one else has a laugh like yours that can bring joy to someone else; and no one else has your experience. Never underestimate how special you are.

> *"Doubt whom you will, but never yourself."*
> Christian Nestell Bovee

SECOND, YOU MUST FIND SHOES THAT FIT

You are complete. You lack nothing. Many times we look at other people and wish that we had something that they possess. Take me for example. I am only 5'4" and I have always wanted to be taller. It is very rare that you won't find me wearing three-inch heels. I had to realize that just because I'm not as tall as someone else, doesn't mean that I am any less of a person. We have been given all the gifts

and talents we need to complete our purpose. Don't worry! If you don't have "it," you don't need "it" to fulfill your destiny. You have everything inside of you that you need to succeed. First, you must believe that you are a whole, complete person, who lacks nothing. You may think that you're not smart enough, but know and believe that you are a total package. You are whole and have everything it takes inside of you to be *great.* You just have to be willing to dig a little deeper to find your greatness.

THIRD, YOUR SHOES MUST BE COMFORTABLE

You have been created to complete a specific task. You have been given a purpose to fulfill on this earth. You may be working in a career that you are good at, but does that mean you're walking in your correct purpose?

It's just like wearing shoes. Shoes are made for walking, but you can't just put any shoe on any foot and expect it to fulfill its purpose. Let's try something. I want you to put this book down right now, and go and get a pair of shoes out of your closet. I'll wait...I have time (SMILE).

You're back? Good. Now, I want you to put your left shoe on your right foot and your right shoe on your left foot. Uncomfortable isn't it? Could you imagine walking around all day like this? You're using the shoes for the "reason" that they were intended, walking around. But oh, how uncomfortable it is when we're not using the shoes in the **correct** way! They are to be used for walking around, but they must be worn on the **correct** foot to fulfill their true purpose. It's just like you and me. Until we build up our self-esteem, we can't walk in the purpose for which we have been created.

Your purpose is why you exist; it is the call on your life. Like vision, your purpose is yours and yours alone. No one else can fulfill your purpose, and you cannot complete someone else's call. Many people wonder how they can find their purpose. But purpose is not something that can be created, it must be discovered. Like vision, your purpose was placed in you before you were born. Discovering your purpose is not as hard as it may sound. It takes time, prayer, soul searching and asking yourself some tough questions. I wake up every day with purpose and on purpose. I no longer wonder why I was put here on this earth. I want you to discover that same feeling, so right now, I want you to quiet yourself, and find a place where you can be alone to think. In the spaces that follow, I want you to write your answers to the following questions. You have to be reflective and meditate upon each question before you answer. You can check out my answers at the end, but no cheating – SMILE!

1. When you were in school what subjects were you able to catch on to faster than your friends?

_____

_____

2. What things do you do well?

_____

_____

3. What games did you enjoy playing as a child?

_____

_____

4. What things do other people say you do well?

_____

_____

5. What are your talents?

_____

_____

6. What do you love doing most?

_____

_____

7. What problems/situations upset you more than anything
else?

_____

_____

MY ANSWERS:

1. I was good at English and History.
2. Writing and speaking.
3. I loved playing "office" and Monopoly.
4. People tell me I speak well.
5. Wow, I have a theme here…I am a good writer and speaker.
6. I love helping other people feel good about themselves.
7. I hate seeing people not doing what they enjoy or what they've been *designed* to do.

Once you've answered these questions, you should begin to see a sketch of what your purpose is in life. Discovering your purpose takes more time than we have here to spend together, but you're off to a great start! Therefore, I want you to keep going even after you finish reading this book!

Many lives will be affected because you have completed the purpose for which you have been destined. That's why you have to believe and accept the truth about yourself - *you are destined to be great!*

Many people are willing to pay a high price for the perfect pair of shoes. Are YOU willing to pay the price that it will take to be great?

Chapter Summary

☐ Self-esteem is needed to discover purpose.

☐ Self-esteem is needed to fulfill purpose.

☐ You are unique - there is no one else like you.

☐ You have everything inside of you that you need to fulfill your purpose.

☐ As you fulfill your purpose, other people's lives are affected.

☐ You are *"A Designer Original."*

Notes:

_____

_____

_____

_____

_____

_____

Prepare to be Fueled by the Wisdom of Leslie Carter

Leslie A. Carter contributes over twenty-five years of progressive leadership experience in client management, career development, coaching and mentoring. As a former Vice President of a fortune 100 health insurance company, Leslie has an extensive professional background. Known as the *leadership connoisseur*, she is the recipient of numerous leadership and recognition awards and was selected to participate in the prestigious Executive Development Leadership Forum. She is also a graduate of Hartford Seminary's Women's Leadership Institute in Connecticut.

As Chief Operating Officer and founder of GGN International Enterprises, Leslie is a Professional Speaker, Business Consultant, Author and Seminar Facilitator. She has worked with several corporate clients and faith-based organizations, delivering each program with quality and a *"spirit of excellence."*

A woman of faith, Leslie is an active servant at Without Walls International Church. She resides in Tampa, Florida with her teenage son.

Website: www.GGNIE.com
Email: Leslie@GGNIE.com
Phone: (813) 885-9717

FUELED BY GREATNESS

MASTERING YOUR MONDAYS

Mondays are days you cannot control. You cannot stop their arrival and you cannot make them go any faster. Each day is 24 hours long, even if it is Monday. So what do we do? How do we master something we can't control? How do we master our Mondays? Well, let's start by looking at some particulars about Mondays.

- Monday is the first business day of the week.

- Most businesses start their pay week on Monday.

- New hires usually start on Monday.

- Major projects and policies are launched on Monday.

- Of the ten federal holidays set by law, five are scheduled on Monday. Martin Luther King, Jr., Day, Presidents' Day, Memorial Day, Labor Day and Columbus Day.

- One popular record company created a website to launch their new artists every Monday.

- "Black Monday" is the name attributed to October 19, 1987. On that day the Dow Jones Industrial Average fell 22.6%, the largest one day decline in recorded stock market history.

- A Japanese study conducted in 2005 indicated that there are 20% more heart attacks on Mondays than on any other day.

- In French, Monday is Lundi representing the moon.

- Monday in Russian is ponedelnik, which means "after do nothing."

- The fourth consecutive million seller song, *Rainy Days and Mondays* was released by the Carpenters in April 1971.

- "Monday morning quarterback" is one who criticizes, passes judgment or states how an event or problem should have been dealt with, after other people have already dealt with it.

- Monday-is a term in pop culture to describe the tired and apathetic feeling many experience upon the return to work after the weekend. It's like having the Monday morning blues.

- According to the American Heart Association, spiritual leaders concerned about health issues in African American and Latino/Hispanic American communities have launched a new initiative called **Search Your Heart Sunday... Go Healthy Monday.** Churches provide heart health messages to their members during Sunday services and encourage them to make healthy changes, beginning Monday, and continuing throughout the week.

- Musical bands, songs, video games, art work, recipes, magazines, books, clubs, poetry, professional sports, even diseases have Monday in their name.

The reality is, depending on your perspective, Mondays could represent a dreadful or exhilarating experience. Yes, Mondays can affect your mood for the week, but they are not just another day of the week. For many of us, Mondays represent stress and change. I once read a statement that said, "without stress there would be no life." Good stress can motivate us, create positive growth, and even make life enjoyable. Bad stress, on the other hand, can cause distress, anxiety, irritability, negative thoughts and reactions.

As the saying goes, "the only constant is change!" The question is how do we manage the stress in our life, the change in our life, the Mondays in our life - how do we *Master Our Mondays?* It starts in the way you see Mondays. Look back on previous Mondays in your life. Did they signify good moments or difficult ones? Generally, do you regret when Sunday evening rolls around and you have to get

ready mentally for Monday? What do you mean master? Master means to take control, conquer, command, ownership, take authority, win, or overcome. You may not have control, but you do have authority! It is how you see and interpret things.

HOW DO YOU MASTER YOUR MONDAY?

YOU FUEL YOUR MONDAY BEFORE YOUR MONDAY STARTS!

Get ready for your week before your week starts. Fuel yourself before your day starts! Fuel your day to expect greatness to be part of your life! Get ready for the stress, obstacle, battle, or situation before you enter into it. You already know its coming. You can foresee the days ahead, so why not get ready to *Master Your Mondays* so that the rest of the week becomes a new and positive challenge? Many of us prepare for our Mondays with prayer and spiritual matters. We find that our weekends are filled with love, family and fellowship. Some people look at Mondays as something to take control of, you're ready to face the week, fueled with the energy to confront and conquer what lies ahead. You say to yourself, "Tuesday's coming - maintain your focus! When Wednesday arrives you say, "Thank God the mid week is already here." Thursdays bring the week to a close ...and when you wake up on Fridays you can say, "I made it!!"

Most of the time we can't change stress but we can change our reaction to it. There are all types of stress that affect us based on our age, gender, socio-economical level, work environment, marital status, parental status, education, neighborhood, school, and the list goes on. Each of us experience our Mondays in different ways, but we can't escape it. Sunday is here and Monday is just around the corner. How do we Master our Mondays? How do we conquer the unconquerable? How do we control the uncontrollable, manage the unmanageable? We *Master our Mondays* through perseverance, resilience, tenacity, fortitude, and endurance. We *Master our Mondays* through a strategy I adopt in my life called:

RSA APPROACH

R = REFOCUS THE VIEW
S = SPHERE OF INFLUENCE
A = ACTION MODE

<u>Refocus The View</u> - **learn to see things through a new lens.**

- Begin to evaluate your thoughts, and become more aware of your surroundings. *Refocusing The View* approach helps you to change your perception to see a new reality. Why is it that two or more people can see the same thing but they react and recall differently? As in the case of witnessing a car accident. Based on your experience and perception, you may interpret the car accident different than another witness. A study conducted by the Journal of Applied Psychology indicated that less that 20% of police witnesses could accurately identify the perpetrators face. Our perception is our reality and no one else's.

- Learn to welcome stress and change in your life. Remove the fear, face the fear, and embrace the change. Begin to conquer those things that previously conquered you.

- Did you know that **<u>STRESSED</u>** spelled backwards spells **<u>DESSERTS?</u>** If you can change your perception, you can change the path you choose. The situation will look different and might even taste different! So as we approach our Mondays we can use a new pair of eyes to refocus the view of the week. Think of good

news - instead of saying, oh no, another Monday, say to yourself, oh yea, another week to be successful!!!

- *Personal Values* impact your family, personal, social, professional, educational, health and financial status. How committed are you to your values? What is most important to you?

Consider ranking the following attributes using a scale from 1 - 10 (1 being the most important)

_____	Security	_____	Weatlth
_____	Service	_____	Independence
_____	Spiritual	_____	Power
_____	Leadership	_____	Relationships
_____	Success	_____	Education

- Upon completion of your ranking, ponder these thoughts - does your life reflect those personal values? How are you demonstrating those values in your day-to-day work? Does your life reflect those values most important to you? Would friends and family agree?

- If you respond "no" to any of those questions, begin to realign your work and play time to reflect your important values. For example, if *service* was ranked as an important value but your days and evenings do not allow for you to serve in your community then you are apt to feel frustrated and unfilled, perhaps not useful. As you identify the values most important to you and align them to your daily schedule, you will begin your week with a fulfilling, rewarding, and positive outlook.

<u>Sphere Of Influence</u> - change what you can, leave the rest alone.

- There are so many things we can change in our life, but we focus so much on the things we cannot change. The *Sphere Of Influence* approach allows you to concentrate your efforts on the things you can change and not worry about the rest. When my family moved to Tampa, Florida in 2005, we heard so many horror stories about hurricanes. After the media coverage of Hurricane Katrina, I remember feeling very uneasy and concerned about our family. We took charge of our fears and began to prepare for a disaster. We met as a family, discussed evacuation plans, created a family contact list, identified a meeting place should we get separated and even purchased perishable items for storage. When Hurricane Wilma arrived a few weeks later, our family felt assured that our action plans would assist us in a crisis. The Tampa Bay area was fortunate that we did not experience a major devastation in the aftermath of Hurricane Wilma.

- Our family had no control of the hurricanes but we did have control on the manner in which we would be prepared to handle the hurricane. We all had a great sense of relief knowing that we were prepared for the worse but prayed for the best. **Mondays can sometimes feel like a hurricane is coming. Prepare now to weather the storm!**

- Be aware of changes, don't mask them, and don't deny them. Make changes before changes make you. Be proactive, instead of reactive to the week ahead. When you begin to feel extremely stressful, identify where it is coming from and begin to reduce the stress. Fuel yourself with energy that is active and positive.

<u>Action Mode</u> - don't wait for life to happen to you, make it happen through you.

- Mastering your Mondays puts you in *Action Mode*. As you approach your week, begin to evaluate the tasks, projects, or accomplishments that need to be completed. Take an active approach to managing your day, week, month and year. We may not be able to control every aspect of our lives but we can take authority over our reactions and the manner in which things impact us. We have the ability to influence our surroundings and change the atmosphere around us. Take an assertive approach to *Mastering Your Mondays*. Life is like a merry-go-round in which time permits no stops. Get fueled up so you are ready to go the distance!

- Before, during, and after the influences come in your life remember you can't <u>change all the stress</u> in your life but can <u>change your reaction to it.</u>

- Utilize the 21 practical principles to Mastering Your Mondays.

TWENTY-ONE PRACTICAL PRINCIPLES OF MASTERING YOUR MONDAYS

1. <u>Plan</u> for the day – get organized. Prepare the night before.

2. <u>Practice</u> choosing your outlook – change your perception. You are responsible for your actions and emotions.

3. <u>Prepare</u> to wait – bring reading materials, give yourself extra time. Set your mind to expect deadlines and get ready for them.

4. <u>Procrastination</u> breeds anxiety and adds unnecessary stress to your life. Whatever you want to do tomorrow, do it today. Whatever you want to do today, do it now.

5. <u>Promise</u> to learn, love, laugh and live. Enjoy life and have fun. Enjoy life, enjoy your successes.

6. <u>Praise Power</u> – for everything that goes wrong, there are probably 10 to 50 things that go right. Begin to count your blessings.

7. <u>Pronounce</u> the word "no" – say "no" to projects and activities that you don't have time for or don't really enjoy.

8. <u>Play</u> quietly – unplug the phone, take a long bath, sleep late, read a novel, enjoy long walks.

9. <u>Physical</u> needs are essential – rest, exercise, sleep well.

10. <u>Pray, Pray, Pray</u> – develop a faith life and expand on it.

11. <u>Put</u> away the chaos – remove the drama from your life. Get organized at work and at home.

12. <u>Paper</u> your thoughts – journal your experiences; it helps to clarify things and provides new perspectives.

13. <u>Pursue</u> positive relationships – surround yourself with people that care for you. Don't be tolerated, be celebrated. Take an inventory of your friends, keep the ones that add to your life.

14. <u>Possess</u> problem resolution mindset – discuss and implement ways to resolve issues and concerns.

15. <u>Personal</u> choices are preferred – what are your preferences: yoga, karate, arts, travel, gardening, music lessons – get a passion.

16. <u>Project</u> your vision – what is your expected outcome? Helen Keller said that "nothing is more tragic than someone who has sight, but has no vision." Where do you want to be, what do you want to do? Start today.

17. <u>Professional</u> help may be necessary – training, coaching, counseling, physican care. If you need help it's okay to get help.

18. <u>Produce</u> the creativity in you – allow your creativity to come out. Everyone is creative, it may not be in music or the arts, but we are all creatures; that denotes we are naturally creative. We've just let life issues silence our creativity.

19. <u>Persevere</u> – don't give up, don't give in. Tomorrow could be the day for your breakthrough. The next person you meet might have the answer. Be persistent through your circumstances. Tomorrow is Tuesday, four days closer to the weekend!

20. <u>Pace</u> yourself – take time to do things right. Reduce the hurried mentality. Plan things but allow for mishaps.

21. <u>Positive</u> attitudes and <u>positive</u> affirmations – the mind affects the body more than any other organ, use it wisely. Be compassionate, be optimistic, be encouraging – to yourself!

Life can be extremely stressful and difficult to manage, but good can come from every situation. When you have a **New** Focus, **New** Commitment and **New** Tools to assist you during those times, you can master anything!

Successfully dealing with change means choosing to grow and develop into an individual that can manage the unmanageable, control the uncontrollable and *Master Your Mondays*. Failing to grow is failing to live. Be committed to yourself. Be deliberate in your actions and thoughts, don't let change take control of you.

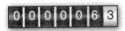

Chapter Summary

☐ Start to *Refocus* Your View - learn to see things through a new lens.

☐ Understand Your *Sphere* of Influence - change what you can, leave the rest alone.

☐ Embrace an *Action* Mode Mentality - don't wait for life to happen to you, make life happen through you.

☐ *Adopt* the 21 practical principles to *Mastering Your Mondays*.

☐ *Plan* ahead so you don't fall back.

Notes:

_____

_____

_____

_____

_____

_____

_____

_____

_____

_____

_____

Prepare to be Fueled by the Wisdom of
Dawnyale Foster

Known as **"The Professional's Cheerleader,"** Dawnyale Foster is a licensed Speech Pathologist. Specializing in the care of the professional speaker, she prepares individuals for media interviews and achieving personal communication goals. As CEO and founder of Fostering Communication, a communications consulting firm, Dawnyale promotes two major areas of the company: improving communication and professional speaking. She motivates audiences using practical principles and powerful keynotes including, "More Than Cheer" and "Becoming a Master Communicator." Dawnyale speaks to diverse groups including businesses and professional organizations, churches, civic groups, primary and secondary schools, colleges and universities.

Dawnyale has mastered the art of successful media communication and shares this specialty with professional and college athletes and cheerleaders. She has developed a model for helping them become *Master Communicators*. As an athlete herself, Dawnyale has enjoyed over 15 years of entertaining football and basketball crowds as a cheerleader. Most recently, she has enjoyed four seasons performing and serving as team captain with the NFL's most entertaining cheerleaders, the 2002 World Champion Tampa Bay Buccaneers Cheerleaders. Whether cheering before 65,000 fans or speaking to audiences of all sizes, Dawnyale is energizing!

Website: www.FosteringYou.com
Email: Info@FosteringYou.com

YOUR BLUEPRINT FOR GREATNESS

When you look up the definition of blueprint, it means a working drawing; a detailed plan for achieving some large undertaking. Keep that definition in mind. Let's think of greatness as something that you want to achieve that will take you to your next level of success. Achieving greatness is a major accomplishment that is unique to each of us, like a promotion, marriage, or possibly even buying or building a home. Now, if we use these definitions for blueprint and greatness, then we could say that *Blueprint For Greatness* means a major plan for achieving your next level. Are you ready to move to your next level? Are you ready to find out how you can build your greatness? Well, greatness requires following a blueprint. This blueprint contains the following five core components to building your foundation for greatness:

CONFIDENCE
SUPPORT
COMMITMENT
A GAME PLAN
WORK

Since blueprints start with these core components, we are what give them uniqueness. What are your gifts and talents? Maybe the uniqueness comes from your personality, networking skills, business sense, or even your humility. We can refer to these qualities as

upgrades or additions to our blueprints. Let me give you an example. When looking at blueprints for houses in a community, you may have three or four basic plans to choose from. But, it is not until each family makes decisions about specific flooring, woodwork, appliances, and other upgrades, that a home actually becomes individualized. These five core components, along with your upgrades, will fuel you for the journey to build your greatness.

Building your *Blueprint For Greatness* starts with **confidence**. I know that your family, friends, teachers, bosses, or co-workers have told you that you need confidence in order to make it in this world. I am here to tell you that they are absolutely RIGHT! **The ME that I want to be always begins with ME!** No one can draw out the greatness in you if it doesn't start with you. You have to believe in yourself first. Think of a person, maybe a family member or friend, who completely drained you because you always had to tell them how great they looked, or how talented they were. Well many of these people lacked self-confidence. If you don't believe in yourself and your abilities, why would you expect others to take a chance on you and trust you with a major project? I am not saying that we will never go through insecure times or lose sight of our goals and purposes, but we need confidence to fuel our journey!

Opportunities are sometimes given to those who display confidence more often than those with the education or experience. Employers would rather train a confident person to do a job than hire someone who has the skills but lacks the confidence. Are you struggling with your self-confidence? If you are, be encouraged and focus on strengthening the first core component of greatness—your confidence. Your fuel source should come from within!

One way you can strengthen your confidence is through positive self-talk. Tell yourself that you are capable of performing that task, signing that major client, and building your greatness. You may have to wake up each morning and look in the mirror and convince

yourself of these things. I know that I have often stared at myself in the bathroom mirror and said, *"I have enough skills to start this company!" "Today I am going to WOW them!" "I am the best person for this position!"* The results were that my self-confidence increased. This process caused me to smile and sometimes even laugh at how funny I thought I looked talking to myself. But, the point is, it worked! So spend a little more time in front of a mirror. Actually, stop reading right now and go to your mirror to practice this self-talk! Say to yourself *"I can make it!"*

> *"Opportunities are sometimes given to those who display confidence more often than those with the education or experience."*

Support is the next core component of your *Blueprint For Greatness!* We all need to have a support system. In life, we are not expected to make it on our own. We need the help and support of others. The old adage says, *"It takes a village to raise a child."* Greatness is sometimes spread, lifted, or boosted by others. I have a support team that consists of family, close friends, and co-workers. I call them my personal cheerleading squad. When I need to be pumped up, energized, cheered on to victory, or kicked back into shape, they are always there. Just as cheerleaders are on the sidelines at football and basketball games yelling out words of encouragement to their team and the fans, your personal squad is doing the same for you. They are usually the loudest, most dedicated, and truthful fans in your individual stadiums of life. That's okay because they are there supporting you!

Learn to openly accept the support of others. Know that your supporters are eager to cheer you on because they care for you and want you to achieve your goals. On the flip side, don't think that your personal cheerleaders will always yell out positive words of encouragement. It is also their responsibility to be your accountability partners, which means telling you things that you may not want to hear. Be willing to listen and accept what they have to say because they have your best interest at heart! Get ready to choose your cheerleading squad to fuel you for your next level of greatness!

Okay, you just read about building your *Blueprint For Greatness* by fueling your confidence and choosing your personal cheerleading squad. Now, let's get ready to make a **commitment.** Do you really want to move forward? If so, how hard are you willing to work to get to greatness? You may have said, *"Oh, I want that so bad that I'll do anything!"* At one point in my life, I only talked about my future goals because I was too afraid to make a commitment to start achieving them. I came to realize that it's not just the talk that's important but also the walk! Don't get stuck on your journey without fuel in your tank. Put in the extra hours, stay late at work, practice and review on your own—basically putting in more than what is expected of you. Remember, greatness always comes at some expense to you. Be willing to give all that you have and then some. As a child, I was taught, "To whom much is given, much is required." I have now learned that I have to use my talents and gifts wisely. So re-evaluate your level of commitment to building your *Blueprint For Greatness.*

Commitment shouldn't only be demonstrated in the presence of others, or when you're in the spotlight. I always wanted to be a secret shopper who went to businesses to evaluate their customer service. If there was a secret shopper at your job, at your church, or civic group watching you, would you be pegged as a dedicated worker, or would your level of commitment be questioned? How much do you give when it appears that no one is looking? From my personal experiences with cheerleading squads, commitment to your team is determined by your attendance at practices and appearances, your performance at rehearsals, and your timeliness. If you were the one who always came to rehearsal two minutes before it started and then didn't know your routines, then your dedication was questioned not only by your leaders but also by your teammates. Remember that when you have more, or want more, you have to give more. **Dedicate yourself to your dedication!** Give more to the activities that you have committed to. Make a pact with yourself that you are going to commit to a task with all that you have and stay true to it! I challenge you to commit yourself today to build your foundation for greatness. Know your limits and remember that to build your greatness you have to be focused, dedicated, and determined. Save your fuel for your major commitments.

> *"Commitment shouldn't only be demonstrated in the presence of others, or when you're in the spotlight."*

Let's recap! So far, you have practiced talking to yourself in your mirror, and started thinking about rearranging your schedule to allow more time to build your greatness. You have also begun embracing your support team. Those action steps are getting you fueled for greatness. Now it's time for you to develop a **game plan**. Your game plan is essential in building your *Blueprint For Greatness.* You need a plan of action! At the beginning of each year people create goals, but most of us struggle with following our goals. What happens? Why are we in the same predicament each year? I want you to develop a habit of writing your goals. Statistics indicate only

5% of people actually write down their goals. But you are going to be different because you have the *Blueprint For Greatness*. When writing your goals, be specific about what you want, how you will master them, and what resources will be needed. Greatness is not built in a day! But greatness requires a carefully designed blueprint.

Know your motives when creating your game plan. Why am I pursuing this goal or job? How will this affect me in the next 5 years? How long will this take me to achieve? How much time, effort, and money will I need to put into my plan? If my plan doesn't work out, what is my back up plan? These are all questions that you should be asking yourself while preparing your game plan.

Be creative in your goal writing, but also remember to be realistic. Don't write a goal that is so far fetched that you can't reach it. When working as a speech pathologist in the school system, I provided speech and language therapy for students. Once a year, I reviewed students' goals, progress, and plans for the next year. Often, I had to remind parents that goals were written to focus on what we wanted to see the students accomplish within a year. If unattainable goals were written, then opportunities for success would be reduced. We all know that we get motivated when we achieve some level of success. So spend some time writing out your game plan to include short and long term goals. Understand that your goals will change several times throughout the process of building your greatness. That's okay!

You have now been fueled by your *Blueprint For Greatness* through **confidence, support, commitment, and developing a game plan.** Don't lose energy now; you're almost there! The last core component to build your foundation for greatness is **work, work,** and more **work!** This is the point where you put the pedal to the metal. You're going to need lots of fuel for this ride. How are you going to work your game plan? As much as we sometimes want the world to be handed to us on a silver platter, greatness is definitely

FUELED BY GREATNESS

not served that way! **Greatness is a monument that is built by the work you do.** Benjamin Franklin once said, *"Never confuse movement with action!"* I was definitely moving around but I was not taking action to achieve my goals. Work is action that creates the results you want!

I encourage you to develop pictures in your mind of the results you want. When I started cheering professionally, I envisioned taking on a leadership role with the squad. During my first two seasons, I observed our team captains, how they led, the skills they possessed, and their responsibilities. I wanted to one day be in one of those positions. So, I developed a game plan. I noted their strengths and their limitations. I also watched how my fellow teammates responded to them. I truly studied them! Then, I got to work! I practiced twice as hard outside of our rehearsals. I agreed to head a committee and I made myself available to help my captains in any way. Remember what you make happen for others, you can make happen for yourself. After being selected for the team a third season, my coordinator asked me to accept the role of team captain. She saw that my work matched my goals. She believed that all I had shown her was enough to successfully lead our team. My blueprint worked for me! Your blueprint will also work for you! Know that if you fuel your game plan with hard work and dedication you're on your way to greatness.

The road to greatness starts with you. The success of your journey to greatness is up to you! Remember to utilize the five core components when building the foundation for your Blueprint For Greatness. Remain diligent, steadfast, and unmovable! Be the biggest fuel source of your Blueprint For Greatness.

"Never confuse movement with action."
Ben Franklin

Chapter Summary

☐ Your *Blueprint For Greatness* is built on the foundation of **confidence, support, commitment, a game plan, and work.**

☐ "The me that I want to be always begins with me."

☐ Dedicate yourself to your dedication.

☐ Greatness is a monument that is built by the work you do.

☐ Know that if you fuel your game plan with hard work and dedication you are on your way to greatness.

Notes:

_____

_____

_____

_____

_____

_____

_____

_____

_____

_____

_____

_____

Prepare to be Fueled by the Wisdom of
Omicron Long

Omicron L. Long is the founder and CEO of *Omicron Long, Inc., a company specializing in youth empowerment.* This engaging and respected speaker is described as a *"Powerhouse"* by nationally known speaker *Delatorro L. McNeal II.*

Mr. Long is an Author, Educator, and Motivator who is a catalyst for the difference in your tomorrow. Omicron is especially active in the fields of children, youth and education, with over 15 years of front-line experience in children's / youth ministry and as a public school teacher. In addition, with nearly ten years of military experience (ranging from communication specialist in West Germany, to duty in *Operation Enduring Freedom* in Afghanistan) he is able to connect with diverse audiences. Omicron continues to serve his country in the U.S. Army Reserve. He has authored several powerful resources including his first motivational book, "It's O.K. to Q.U.I.T: For Anyone Who Has Ever Thought About Giving Up." Mr. Long's relevant and humorous presentations will deliver understanding, challenge and change to your audience.

Website: www.OmicronLong.com
Email: Info@OmicronLong.com
Phone: (813) 240-3542

IT'S O.K. TO QUIT

A Life Story

A farmer and his dog were working together in a pasture. Later that afternoon, a rabbit suddenly appeared and the *chase* began. The furry little mammal shot out like a cannonball and moved like lightning. At first, the frightened animal ran straight, then zigzagged, then bounced, and all this was done with a passion and desperation that belied the animal's inherent cuteness. The hound was on the rabbit's tail, and, though this hunter was a strong and agile beast still in his prime, the canine looked helpless, if not foolish, as he slid and braked, twisted and turned trying to keep up with the fantastic and furious maze that instinct had patterned into the mind of the hunted.

After a mere two minutes the hound, weary and beyond exhaustion, stopped. The rabbit found safety by firing himself into a thicket of briars and vines. The dog's mouth was open, and sweet cherished oxygen was being processed from the air as quickly as his heart and lungs could operate. The man, smiling smugly, said to his old companion, "Well, I guess I know who's better...I saw who won the battle today." The dog listened, and it became very quiet. Now, all that was heard were the soft, slowing pants of the animal, gradually catching his breath. Then, slowly raising his head to meet the self-satisfied gaze of the farmer's eyes, the hound addressed his longtime master and friend. With an authority earned through years of competition on nature's battlefield, he said "Farmer, your eyes showed you many things, but what they failed to show you was the power and motivation behind the battle." "Sir, to me, today's contest was just for fun, for laughs, or, perhaps a lunch," but for that rabbit, for him old friend...*it was for life."*

What are you doing as you process **your** oxygen? Is what you're doing for laughs, you know just passing the time, something to do? Maybe it's lunch, that which enables you to support yourself and possibly even provide for others. If not, then is it **life,** your very heartbeat, a life you believe in? Are you getting the results you want in life, are you making a difference? The outcome of *the chase* was determined, in fact *predetermined* by each participant's *determination.* **One had no chance, because the other had no choice.**

Is there a dream, a goal, something you've desired in the past, or planned for the future? Do you have the motivation that you need to reach that dream? In life are you the rabbit, or the dog? Are you the bug, or the windshield? Are you the put-up or the shut-up? Do you have the absolute determination to get to your goals and even get *back* up if necessary? In the chase the dog's motivation was weak: laughs or lunch, and no matter what happened, the farmer would feed him that night. He had a **way out.** The rabbit's **motivation** was **fueled** by his very **life,** his passion for existence. **You and I must have solid, powerful, hi-octane reasons to motivate us to reach our dreams.**

THE QUESTION TO THE ANSWER

When we put our time, energy, money, our life into a goal, it should to be worthwhile. It is **extremely** important that you and I understand the reasons behind what we are doing because that is what will **drive** and sustain us as we strive toward our goal.

It's the question to the answer...why? An example: are you exercising to lose weight *so people can see you on their wedding day fit into those clothes,* or are you getting in better physical condition for your *own health?* **It is important that the *reason be your* own.** If what you are doing is to ultimately please anyone but yourself you will possibly set yourself up for disappointment. If your relationship falters or

changes in any way then so does your motivation because of an inferior and corrupt reason. **Do what you do ultimately to satisfy yourself.**

Though part of making a decision is your heart (your inner self), make sure that good solid judgment is included in the formula throughout the entire process. Get wise counsel from many different places, people, and mentors. Ask questions. Do research. You don't have to use all of the advice you get, but, do carefully consider the findings and feedback you get. This chapter is a prime example. Take what you need, what fits, what works for you, and as the old saying goes, "Chew the hay and spit out the sticks." To ultimately stay the course and not quit, your reason must be a worthy one, not corrupt, a whim or a passing fad. If your reasons are worthy, your motive will be sound, and then truly, you are being fueled by greatness.

Here are 7 Questions to Ponder When Pursuing Your Dream

1. *Why am I doing this, why do I want to reach my goals and achieve this dream?*

2. *Will achieving this dream help me, or will it hurt me?*

3. *Will achieving this dream help others or will it hurt anyone else?*

4. *Do I know what achieving these goals will cost (in money, time, and effort)? Am I willing to pay the price?*

5. *Does it matter if everyone knows what I am doing, or if no one knows what I am doing? Will either change what I do?*

6. *Will I ever be sorry that I went for my dreams, or instead will I regret that I didn't?*

7. *What will I do if I fail at my attempt(s), to reach my dream, will I quit?*

...TO QUIT ?

Will you quit? People of planet Earth are notorious quitters. We brag about it, fantasize about it, write songs about it. Johnny Paycheck's song *"Take this job and shove it..."* has become part of the fabric of Americana. We quit schools, clubs, churches, marriages, teams and dreams. We quit trying, praying, searching, giving, living and we decide to simply survive. We quit on ourselves and it wouldn't be quite so big a problem if it only hurt one person, but as Bill Wilson of *Metro Ministries International*™ reminds us, *"Nobody Quits Alone."* Somebody's watching you whether you know it or not. They are rooting for you and they want to see you succeed, because they say to themselves, "if they can do it, then so can I." But as bad as quitting can be, there are times when quitting is right; there are some things that it's o.k. to quit.

<u>Here are Seven Things that It's O.K. to Quit.</u>

1. *It's O.K. to quit* **sitting around on our** *"buts."* People say "but I can't do this, or I don't have that." We're waiting on the tooth fairy, the lottery, or a pot of gold at the end of the rainbow. I personally have been susceptible to paralysis of analysis, which is sitting and looking and thinking instead of doing. There will always be "buts" or excuses not do something. *Sometimes we have to leap before we look.* This is not a license to act foolishly, but it is permission to try. Don't worry about making mistakes or failing because if you want to be successful, mistakes and failure are both part of the process.

2. *It's O.K. to quit* **complaining.** I have been on four of Earth's seven continents and to over a dozen countries so I'll tell you first hand that if you are able to **read** this, you are blessed. If you were able to **buy** this book, if you can study this in a **warm** decent place, and have **eaten** at least once today, if you can even mention that you are blessed or anything referring to God at all **without fear of persecution or death**...you are blessed.

3. *It's O.K. to quit* expecting something for nothing. Sometimes we wish some things were easier than they are. *We want a Saks Fifth Ave.*™ *life at a Kmart*™ *price.* But, more often than not, *we must really put in first-class work, for first-class results.* You get what you pay for. You don't get something for nothing. *You reap what you sow (Galatians 6:9).* These phrases all tell us the same thing. **They don't tell us to quit dreaming, but to stop simply fantasizing and put some actions to our dreams.**

4. *It's O.K. to quit* **doing the same stupid things** that got us in trouble, or got us nowhere the last time. **If we want different results, we must take different actions.** The quote is *"stupid is as stupid does," Professor* Forrest Gump™ said that, not Albert Einstein. We've all heard that Einstein had shortcomings, but we also *know* of his achievements. The exact same batter that strikes-out, also produces the home run, when they focus and remember **lessons learned** from their last time at bat.

5. *It's O.K. to quit* **looking for the spectacular, while ignoring simple solutions.** Many times we want the Hollywood effect in our lives and we miss the *common sense solutions.* Once I was trying to diagnose some car trouble and my hood was up. My next door neighbor (a teenager) said to me *"Mr. O,(A nickname for Omicron) it's your battery."* I'm thinking, this guy was probably raised by a family of mechanics and drinks oil for breakfast. He can probably tell the problem just by hearing the improper hum of the alternator belt" or he can smell the weak mixture of battery acid in the air as the engine runs. So I casually said *"Yeah, how do you know…?"* He replied *"Well this is the second day in a row you've had to get your car jumped."* I bought a new battery within the hour, problem solved. *Simple not spectacular.*

ALERT!!! PAY ATTENTION, THIS ONE CAN COST YOU EVERYTHING!

6. *It's O.K. to quit hanging around* people who are no good for you. <u>*There are people in your life who cannot and will not go with you on your way to your dream.*</u> People will either help take you up or drag you down, there is **no neutral. Think.** You know who these people are in your life, and you know the reasons they are bad for you. Did you know that just a few drops of water or **contaminate** in the **fuel** will stop a multi-million dollar high performance race car, cold? Many persons we call friends are actually just acquaintances who will leave you when the times are tough. **Think,** are these toxic associations worth **your life's dream?** *There are a lot of fish in the sea, and you get to stock your own aquarium.*

7. *It's O.K. to quit* blaming everyone and everything else for things that we have control or influence in. Stop being a victim. **We can't always control what happens to us, but we can control how we respond to it.** I love the epic TV mini-series Roots. There is a scene in episode one in which Lavar Burton as Kunte Kinte and Ji-Tu Cumbuka as *The Wrestler* are chained below deck with dozens of other captive African slaves. In the scene, the young Kunte Kinte cries out in desperation and rage *"Allah (his god) will save us!"* The older and wiser *Wrestler* replies that *"Allah* **made** us warriors, he gave us the ability, we must save ourselves." **What have you been given the ability to do?**

What is one thing that you are going to "Quit" right now?
What will accelerate your life?

_____

_____

_____

_____

_____

_____

TO BE OR NOT TO BE...? THAT IS THE QUESTION

A class was discussing the Second Amendments *right to bear arms.* They wondered if restricting those rights (like some European countries do), would deter crime in the U.S. They concluded that once people have decided to become involved in crime (even with the threat of the death penalty) it is almost impossible to stop them. Sooner or later, a person will find a way. This determination and **"I will not be stopped," attitude** if used for good, is the mindset of a winner, a champion. This is the great unstoppable force and also the immovable object. This is you and I when the **reason is right,** when we really **want to do or to be.**

The Spanish explorer Hernando Cortez had a goal. He had a small army of soldiers; numerous were afraid, many were tired and home sick, morale was low and some were threatening **to quit,** to take the ships and leave, instead of facing the many hardships, including their enemy, in battle. The *legend* says that Cortez, to avoid giving his men **a way out,** set fire to these vessels which were their means of retreat and escape.   So a now highly motivated army was fighting, and though vastly outnumbered by the Aztecs and having lost some battles, they won the war. <u>Cortez's enemies, obstacles, and challenges **had no chance, because Cortez had no choice.**</u>

On the **streets** of your success, you may have read numerous books and heard many great speakers or stories concerning reaching your goals and dreams. However, if you've allowed yourself a way out, an **avenue** of escape, you *may* never reach your destination.   But when you *demonstrate* strong motives, and *determine* to **quit** that which holds you back, and **when you** display an "I will not be stopped" attitude, and **decide, "I have no other choice,"** then your excuses and obstacles will fall, because then, you are truly being **Fueled by Greatness.**   Which **road** will you choose?

More Power To Ya!

Chapter Summary

☐ The strength of our motivation is determined by the strength of our reasons.

☐ Our reason should be worthy and ultimately self satisfying.

☐ There are seven areas to consider when pursuing your dream.

☐ Often quitting is the wrong thing to do, but sometimes it's O.K. to quit.

☐ If we give ourselves no other choice, our obstacles have no chance.

Notes:

_____

_____

_____

_____

_____

_____

_____

_____

_____

_____

_____

_____

_____

Prepare to be Fueled by the Wisdom of

Kim Johnson

Kim Johnson is a Professional Speaker and Wellness Consultant. She educates, empowers, inspires and instructs audiences worldwide to pursue a life of greatness through total wellness. Known fondly as *"The Wellness Nurse,"* her ability to present wellness in an achievable way has led to a decrease in our nation's crisis in health.

Her passion and purpose for health will empower you to make lifestyle changes immediately that will ensure lasting wellness results. As a sought after professional speaker she delivers her signature keynote, *"Pass the Pudding for Health,"* to profit and nonprofit organizations, churches and schools. Her keynote has been said to be *"the most needed and practical information"* for this age.

As President and CEO of *Choose Health Today, Inc.* she is a life changing wellness consultant, teacher and successful entrepreneur. Kim is dedicated to equipping people to live in total wellness including their mind, body, spirit, finances, and relationships. Audiences across the nation rave that she is the *"TOTAL WELLNESS EXPERT"* who will leave you empowered to walk in your God-given right of wellness.

Website: www.KimJohnson.org
Email: Info@KimJohnson.org
Phone: (912) 729-5925

TOTAL WELLNESS FOR GREATNESS
Living Everyday Well

> *"Total wellness starts in the mind, stimulates the body, stirs the spirit, seizes the environment and shares with others the spectacular ability to live, love and learn."*
> Kim Johnson

A typical day for me as a nurse is taking care of people from all walks of life who are not well. Their bodies are broken, their minds are confused, their spirits are down and they are struggling in their relationships. This daily encounter of working with people, not walking in wellness has led me to my own pursuit of **total wellness** and to assist as many people as I can to walk in total wellness. I have found, through my encounters and experiences, that total wellness is achieved only when your mind, body, spirit and relationships are whole. Ask yourself the following questions. *Are you mentally challenged? Do you need a checkup from your feet up? Are the relationships in your life in need of a heart transplant? Do your finances need major surgery? Does your spirit soar or are you bedridden?* If so, grab a pen and paper and walk with me as I fuel you through five proven principles that will serve as a framework for total wellness. **Are you ready?**

Let's go!

TOTAL WELLNESS PRINCIPLE #1:
TOTAL WELLNESS STARTS IN THE MIND!

What you perceive is what you will achieve, so perceive wellness. Your mind is an awesome tool! When stimulated properly it can push you towards your destiny. You have to develop strategies for stimulating your mind. Below are some suggestions to get you started.

- Constantly feed your mind with positive affirmations and data.
- Guard your mind from negative thoughts.
- Challenge your mind with new ideas and situations.

Most battles start in the mind. So start inputting positive data and releasing negative data.

TOTAL WELLNESS PRINCIPLE #2:
TOTAL WELLNESS STIMULATES THE BODY!

Your health is the backbone of your career, family, finances and relationships. Yes, it's that important! Winning at health is an obtainable goal. Let me share with you some tools that will assist you in total wellness in your body. Let's start by practicing the mind principle. Say with me, **"I can and will obtain Total Wellness in Health."** Did you mean it? If not, repeat it again and again until your mind and body can believe and receive the connection. Remember total wellness starts in the mind and then it stimulates the body. **Wellness is obtainable and YOU can obtain it.** Statistics and critics of our day would have you believe that it's not obtainable. Many people feel they have to try every new diet and fad that comes along in order to walk in total wellness. These fads are not the way

to go. Take a look at these statistics and you decide if quick fixes are creating the changes we need.

- Heart Disease is the number one killer in America.
- Cancer rates are on the rise and may even surpass Heart Disease.
- Over 20 million Americans have Diabetes.

You don't have to be consumed with your eating habits every moment of the day, you just have to put some key principles in place and follow them. There are *no quick fixes* when it comes to your health; there is no fad or current trend that will lead to lasting results. Contrary to current ads, unhealthy trends of consuming increased fat through fast food, increased sugar consumption and lack of exercise are not the norm for a person pursing greatness. You must change your mind, your habits, and make better choices towards wellness daily.

Remember, **"When You're Healthy Everybody Wins!"**

Get to know your body, and take time to learn how your body functions.

- Find out how your body responds to certain types of foods.
- Examine how much energy you have before and after you eat certain foods.
- Check your emotional level before and after meals.
- Determine if your diet is in line with your goals and plans and if it's contributing to your body's needs.

When you take the time to listen to your body and make the necessary changes to monitor your energy level and pursue wellness, your body will reward you with what you need to reach your goals. Utilize P.U.D.D.I.N.G. as a tool to assist you with this principle.

P = portion control
U = utilize resources
D = downsize
D = decisions
I = increase
N = no
G = get moving

Let's examine this tool a little more closely. Statistics say that the average American **P**ortion size is two to three times larger than most civilized countries. I found that unless you want to be two to three times as large, watch your portions. When **U**tilizing your resources, you need to educate yourself on the benefit of certain foods, for instance fruits and vegetables are known to decrease your cancer risk by thirty percent. However not all fruits and vegetables are equal. Choose dark leafy vegetables and go for more colorful fruits. *D*ownsizing is never fun. When it comes to your health you must downsize your intake of non-nutritional foods, eat them sparingly. Our over consumption of these foods has gotten us the title of the **land of the fat!** The second D is for **D**ecisions. You have to decide that your health is a priority and then make small changes daily towards wellness. No one can make that decision for you or make your health better but you. I is for **I**ncrease and you must increase your knowledge on ways to enhance your overall health, through incorporating proven practices. Watch your salt intake, grill foods instead of frying, cook at home versus eating out. N is for no. Say it with me, **"NO!"** Say no to overeating and restaurants that don't give you a choice for wellness. Say no to foods that rob your energy and hinders your goals towards wellness. G is for **G**et moving. The World Health Organization states that two thirds of the illnesses that lead to death are related to our diet and lack of exercise.

GET MOVING!

FUELED BY GREATNESS

Here are a few tips to get you moving:

- Schedule your exercise first thing in the morning.
- Break up your exercise into ten minutes segments three times a day.
- March in place during commercial breaks.
- Take the stairs when available.
- Enroll in a dance class.

Remember you have to expend energy to get energy.

Utilize the tool of P.U.D.D.I.N.G as one of your total wellness tools. Eating foods that are nutritionally poor one or two times will not upset your goals and plans for your life. Consistently choosing foods that have very little nutritional value and eating them in large quantities will surely lead to detours on your road to total wellness.

TOTAL WELLNESS PRINCIPLE #3:
TOTAL WELLNESS STIRS THE SPIRIT!

Your spirit, like your mind, needs to be fueled constantly. Winning in your spirit and walking in total wellness requires awareness of your emotions. Your emotions have a way of either brightening or darkening your days. Ask yourself, *"Do I have control of my emotions or are my emotions controlling me?"* There are many ways to fuel your spirit. Music is a way of enhancing your emotions for the good. The next time you need a boost in your spirit put on your favorite song and feed your spirit. Statistics show that colors can change the way we think and behave. Brighten up your day with colors. Bright colors play a major role in your attitude and emotions. Choose colors that are invigorating that remind you of special places or things like the sunshine, the ocean or even the rainbow. **What color is your spirit?** What color comes to mind when you think of yourself? Red, black, blue, yellow? Does this color represent you well, or do you need a color change?

Your spirit is very important because it's where your inner core lives, your inner self. When properly fueled, the inner you will lead to a powerful outer you. If you have troubles with your inner core, seek wise counseling. Sometimes past hurts and failures need professional attention. I encourage you to take whatever steps are necessary to walk in *total wellness* from your inner self to your outer self. Total wellness is inner driven. Find ways to bring it out through prayer, praise, worship and thanksgiving. If your inner self is not well, then you are not well. Work diligently on your inner core. Here are a few suggestions:

- **Control your emotions.**
- **Stop negative self talk immediately.**
- **Receive and apply constructive feedback.**
- **Take the necessary steps to make positive changes so that you know and love yourself from the inside out.**

When you take these steps you will find you are on your way to letting your spirit soar.

*Okay are you still walking with me? Any questions or comments? Email me at **Info@kimjohnson.org** and I will send you Wellness Tips on any topic discussed in this chapter.*

TOTAL WELLNESS PRINCIPLE # 4:
TOTAL WELLNESS SEIZES
THE ENVIRONMENT!

Is your environment serving you well? Your total wellness will thrive only if you *seize* your environment. Seizing your environment is predicated upon you Purposefully Living Above the Norm (P.L.A.N). I sense that you are already living above the norm, because you are taking the time to read this book that can cut your learning curve. Does your environment make inferences? Are these inferences effecting you positively or negatively? If you have a plan then you will thrive in any surrounding. Let's look at one way your environment might be influencing you. Television commercials and billboards are telling us that it's okay to spend, spend, and spend. Adopting this attitude will cost you in your pursuit of total wellness. You have to decide how best to spend your finances and not be influenced by your environment. You are worth the effort and discipline it takes to have total wellness in your finances. Don't be financially illiterate.

Take a look at the following statistics and decide if you will follow your environment.

- The average American is carrying over $8,000 in consumer debt.
- One out of every three households has a second mortgage on their home.
- Statistics say that the average American has no emergency fund or plan, if they were to lose their job.
- Most Americans have borrowed against their retirement plan or don't contribute to one at all.

Does this sound like a fortified environment?
If not, *SEIZE IT* and *SEIZE IT NOW!*

How do you build a fortified environment? By having a plan and sticking with it. Surround yourself with financial tools. Utilize a financial planner, research investment opportunities at your financial level. Make wise choices when you are spending your money. *RESPECT YOUR MONEY.* Ask yourself the following questions. Is this purchase needed? Is it needed right now? Can I afford it? If you answer no to any of these questions then don't use your hard earned cash for this purchase. Your environment can slow, stop or hinder you in your pursuit of total wellness. Your financial environment is one of the major ways to hinder your total wellness. *Don't Let It!* Examine your environment for growth factors.

Is your environment conducive for growth? Are there proper schools for advancing your education? Are there progressive employment opportunities available to you? Do you feel safe in your environment? You have to seize your environment for total wellness. Take daily purposeful movements to improve your environment.

**WELLNESS PRINCIPLE #5:
TOTAL WELLNESS ENHANCES
YOUR RELATIONSHIPS!**

I purposely saved total wellness in relationships as the last principle. The other four principles have to be implemented and given some serious thought before you can have total wellness in your relationships. If your mind, body, spirit, and environment are not whole, your relationships will suffer. Building lasting relationships takes time. Taking the time to build relationships that are built on trust and mutual respect will give you opportunities to walk in total wellness in your relationships. People in your life who are making positive deposits are gifts to be cherished. When pursing total wellness in your relationships incorporate these tools:

Take the time to listen attentively.

- Appreciate the unique qualities of each individual.
- Strive to live peacefully with others.
- Love others as you love yourself.

FUELED BY GREATNESS

These tools will empower you to *laugh* without hypocrisy, *love* without restraints, and *live* without fear of failure.

When pursuing total wellness for greatness, I encourage you to **ALWAYS CHOOSE EXCELLENCE!**

- Choose excellence in your mindset and emotions.
- Choose excellence in your body.
- Choose excellence in your environment.
- Choose excellence in your relationships.

You are now fueled to walk in TOTAL WELLNESS. WILL YOU?

Here's my **30 day Total Wellness Challenge** for you:

1. Develop 5 positive affirmations and repeat them daily.
2. After getting approval from your healthcare professional incorporate 30 minutes of exercise into your daily schedule.
3. For the next 30 days journal your days events and ways to improve yourself from the inside out.
4. Learn one new financial term or principle a day and apply it to your financial environment.
5. In the next 30 days I want you to genuinely compliment at least one person daily.

Chapter Summary

☐ Your mind starts your journey to total wellness.
☐ Total Wellness in your health is obtainable.
☐ If your inner self is not well then you are not well.
☐ Have a plan and seize your environment.
☐ Building healthy relationships start with you being whole first.

Notes:

_____

_____

_____

_____

_____

_____

_____

_____

_____

_____

_____

_____

Prepare to be Fueled by the Wisdom of Jorgie Franks

Jorgie Franks is the CEO and founder of *Taylor Made Me, Inc*. She is a Professional Speaker, Spokesmodel, Success Coach, and Author. Jorgie educates and empowers you to avoid making excuses about why you have not achieved your goals. If you want to be successful you have to let your goals consume you and limit distractions.

Jorgie Franks is currently one of the top 5 speakers for the largest modeling and acting school in the country, BARBIZON. At age 24 she wrote the book, <u>You Goal Girl!: The Ultimate Guide to Achieve All Your Goals</u>. Pam Iorio, the mayor of the city of Tampa endorses the book saying, "You Goal Girl offers inspiring motivation for women of all ages-a must read."

Jorgie earned her bachelor's degree in Interpersonal and Organizational Communication at The University of South Florida. She is energetic, vivacious and full of power. Her mission is to make a connection and change lives. Her keynotes include, "You Go!" "You Goal Girl" and "Excuses...Excuses." Jorgie Franks, also known as, "The Goal Girl," is a wonderful speaker and can challenge any audience to stop making excuses and achieve their destiny.

Website: www.JorgieFranks.com
Email: Jorgiez@aol.com

WHEN GREATNESS IS YOUR GOAL

"Greatness involves self-evaluation."

Greatness is determined by your opinion of yourself, not by others' opinion of you. Most people have no idea how to act when greatness is their goal. When I visit schools, churches, and corporate environments daily I hear a lot of ideas when it comes to greatness. Some think paychecks determine greatness and others think your grade point average determines greatness. What do you think determines greatness?

Greatness is when you excel above others without comparing yourself to others. Greatness is not ordinary; it is taking your goals to the next level and setting yourself apart. Greatness is doing ordinary things extraordinarily well. Greatness is not just being you, it is being the best you. It is fulfilling what you were born to do.

Look at yourself and weigh your position. Maybe you should be taking notes. Where are you in your journey to your goal: greatness? Do you need an attitude adjustment? Are you a negative person? Do you dress for success? Are you arrogant or humble? Regarding finances, what are your strengths and what are your weaknesses? Who are your friends? Do you have any friends? Do you volunteer? Is your house clean? Do you encourage others? Do you get rest? Are you organized? Do you ask for help? Are you letting others distract you from your goals?

There are a lot of different areas you need to adjust to reach greatness in your life. You may be great in some areas but weak in others. The long-term goal in your life is greatness. You want to be

the best you can be and that is why you set short-term goals to strengthen the areas in which you are weak. As you ask yourself the questions above you may already be thinking about ways you can improve. Write down these ideas. What are some goals you can set to reach that extraordinary level called greatness?

I refer to eight types of goals in depth in, "You Goal Girl!: The Ultimate Guide to Achieve All Your Goals."

The types of goals I refer to are:
1. Finances
2. Personal Development
3. Relationships
4. Extracurricular activities, professional organizations, volunteer work
5. House cleaning
6. Physical health
7. Spirituality
8. Quality time in your relationships.

I am sure you can think of several other types of goals you can make on your goal to greatness.

8 SHORT-TERM GOALS TO REACH YOUR LONG-TERM GOAL: GREATNESS

1. When Greatness is Your Goal You Are Always Growing. Fear and self-doubt can stifle your growth. Dedicate yourself to baby steps to overcome your fear.

Real Life Application: My youngest brother is a Christian rapper. He is extremely dedicated to his work. I noticed he would sit in his room for hours writing songs and making beats. First, I bought him a digital voice recorder so he could hear himself. Then I challenged him to perform in front of family and friends. He was nervous at first

but after awhile he did not mind. Everyone saw he had a powerful gift. After he mastered small groups I introduced him to larger forums. I took him to the studio and now he performs in front of hundreds. He realized his own greatness and now he is on the journey towards excellence. He wants more songs and his own clothing line. He wants to produce a CD and hire a manager.

2. When Greatness is Your Goal You Persevere Over Obstacles. When people say life is hard I cannot help but agree. It seems like as soon as you feel like you are comfortable another challenge comes. The Bible says in 1 Peter 5:10, *"After you suffer a little while, God will restore you and make you strong, firm, and steadfast."* Do not worry because your strength is coming. It may not come when you want it but it will arrive on time. Salvation is essential to Greatness.

Real Life Application: Usually, it is not evident to outsiders when I am going through trying times because of my positive attitude. In my younger years I did not understand genuine joy so I faked it, but now it is real. I have developed a support group I can trust. I have developed a relationship with Jesus Christ and I cannot be great without Jesus. When I feel like I have made a big mistake, I always have my loved ones to help me get through.

3. When Greatness is Your Goal You Do Not Make Excuses. By creating excuses for your shortcomings you are holding yourself back. It is hard to eliminate excuses from your life, but to be great you must accept responsibility for your life and decisions. When you make mistakes people do not want to hear excuses.

Real Life Application: As a speaker who talks to middle and high school students' everyday, I have found some very basic ways to explain the effect of excuses. Motivational Speaker and Author, Anwar Richardson states that there are 7 dangers of excuses.
1. "It is a built-in reason for failure." If you come to class without your homework, you get an F. F equals failure.

The excuse would be you left it on the counter. Now you have a reason for your failure. Excuses are a built in reason for failure.

2. "It deflects all blame." We blame the alarm clock when we are late. We blame our parents when we have defects. Students blame the teacher when they have a C. We have to accept responsibility.

3. "It allows you to become inferior." The Lord will make you the head and not the tail. Read Deuteronomy 28:13. If you make excuses it is contradictory to God's will for your life.

4. "It forces you to admit defeat." Romans 8:37 reads, *"We are more than conquerors through him who loved us."* Fight for your destiny. Think of all the reasons you should have hope.

5. "People do not value your word." No one believes you anymore. You slowly lose your integrity and character which are essential to greatness. People feel they cannot depend on you because you continue to make excuses. Most people equate excuses with something negative or a lie.

6. "It turns average into a lifestyle." I call this out in almost every school I visit. In basic terminology average is settling. Average is when you choose not to challenge yourself to achieve greatness. Average is the minimum you can do to get by. When I was in school I made average my lifestyle academically. I excelled in popularity and sports but when it came to academics, I was very much average. And I find that average gets you below average results. That really hit home when I tried to get into University of South Florida and got rejected. When I was ready to move out, I had to live at home with my parents because I did not have the money. I had no options and I was in debt. I am still paying for

college. Every month on the 17th, I pay $72.95, for the next 10 years. That is what average will get you. Now I choose not to settle in any areas of life.

7. _"It convinces everyone, including yourself, that you're not an achiever."_ Visualize the last time you came to work late. Most likely, all the way to work, you are thinking of an excuse. What will it be today? Will I say it was the train, the kids, the husband, wife, or maybe you were not feeling well. You get to work late and say your son wouldn't cooperate. Now you have convinced yourself and the boss you cannot achieve the simple task of getting to work on time.

4. When Greatness is Your Goal You Must Serve. The Bible states in Luke 9:46-50 that if you want to be great you must first be a servant. Have you ever noticed how most people who are considered great have had a very humble beginning? Can you think of your mentors? How did they get their start?

Real Life Application: Oprah Winfrey is a woman who is considered great but she started out humbly. Her unmarried parents split when she was very young. She had to live with her grandmother. She did not get her first pair of shoes until she was six. She was molested and became a teenage mother from one of her abusers. Her child died after birth. Oprah overcame her humble beginning to become the only African-American woman to ever make Forbes' billionaire list.

5. When Greatness is Your Goal You Minimize Distractions. I used to believe that if you allow your goals to consume you there is no way you cannot achieve them. This may be true but a distraction can take you off course. If your goal is being great you must minimize distractions. Distractions come as men or women, or even something like music, TV, or shopping. If I told you one distraction could keep you from your destiny would you let it go? What are your distractions?

Real Life Application: My distractions came from the opposite sex. When I graduated with my Associate's degree in Mass Communications I got involved with a man who totally re-arranged my life. My goals to be involved in school and do these great feats at church were postponed because this beautiful man who seemed to have all the answers distracted me. Imagine my surprise when I ended up pregnant and he was gone when our daughter was 2 months old. I thank God for my beautiful daughter but surely I could have gone without the distraction. That relationship made me realize that to be great you have to minimize distractions.

6. **When Greatness is Your Goal You Dress the Part.** The way we dress communicates before we even open our mouth. Ask yourself the question, "Does my attire communicate Greatness?"

Real Life Application: Working for the largest modeling and acting center in the country was new to me. I was not used to being referred to as a spokesmodel. When I tell people who my corporate sponsor is they expect the image. I literally remember apologizing for my attire. I was at a casual event representing Barbizon and I felt like I was not dressed as well as everyone there. I decided I would never apologize again. I hired an image consultant and now I don't have to worry about people asking me if I am a model. They just know.

7. **When Greatness is Your Goal You Surround Yourself with Positive People Who Say Positive Things.** People around you should bring you up and support your dreams. I would go out on a limb and say the more positive people you have around you, the more positive you will be.

Real Life Application: Here are some important questions to ask yourself when choosing those closest to you: Are they there during the good and the bad? How bad do they talk about others (Because they will talk about you)? Are they an attribute to others in their life? Are you saying positive things about others? What can you say positive to encourage yourself? Since you are making goals that will impact your life, you want to make sure they are protected by surrounding yourself with a positive support team. Who are the positive people in your life?

8. **When Greatness is Your Goal Develop a Written Plan of Action.** Put your goals everywhere and be creative. Make goal setting fun for you. You must write your goals to hold yourself accountable. You must have vision for your life to make goals possible.

Real Life Application:
Long-Term goals ask these questions:
- What do you want in the future?
- Why do you want to achieve this goal?
- How important is this goal to you?
- What will be the effect if you do not achieve this goal?

Short-Term goals ask these questions:
- What are you doing to get your long-term goals?
- Is there more than one thing you can do right now to insure your success?

Daily goals ask these questions:
- What can I do today to get closer to completing these short-term goals?
- Am I using my time wisely?

This is your life so you better take it seriously. You are great and it is your duty to fulfill your God-given gifts. Don't look back over your life, years down the road, and have regrets for the questions you did not answer. You need to be able to defend yourself and your decisions. Greatness involves self-evaluation.

CHAPTER NINE

When Greatness is Your Goal — *Jorgie Franks*

Chapter Summary

- ☐ Greatness involves evaluating yourself and confronting your weaknesses.
- ☐ You must set different types of goals to reach greatness and improve your weaknesses.
- ☐ When greatness is your long-term goal there are seven short-term goals you must apply to your life.
- ☐ You have the ability to become great. Greatness is not just being you, it is being the best you.
- ☐ Greatness is a life long journey upward.

Notes:

_____

_____

_____

_____

_____

_____

_____

_____

_____

_____

_____

Dr. Loleta Wood Foster has a **spirited passion for the power of communication and relationships**. She has spoken before thousands and led countless seminars, workshops and training programs. She has also successfully coached more than one thousand individuals, teams, couples and families in **the art of using intentional acts** to bring about the outcomes they desire. **You'll learn the power of adding extra to your ordinary** from her expertise, stories, and strategies for success.

Dr. Foster is a Professional Speaker, Leader, Psychologist, Educator, Weekly TV Host, Facilitator, Author and Life Coach, who walks her talk. She is a **2002 recipient of the prestigious ATHENA Award**, honoring individuals who strive toward the highest levels of professional excellence. Acknowledged by others as **"The Voice of Reason,"** Dr. Foster has her B.A. and Master's degrees in Speech Pathology and a Ph.D. in Psychology.

She is excited about spreading her views in her new books, Wake Up and Go For It! – An End to Sleepliving! and Connecting With Ourselves and Others.

WAKE UP AND GO FOR IT!

When I was a child, I was fascinated by the concept of sleepwalking. I must have seen something on a television show or movie about someone sleepwalking. Why couldn't they just wake up? Would they walk outside during the night? But what would they do, if they'd just wake up and find themselves out of their beds? I would let my imagination run wild and before I knew it, I would be afraid that one day I would find myself sleepwalking. You get the picture! Who would want to have to deal with that affliction?

Well, let's look at sleepwalking in a different way. Think about whether there have been times in your life when you felt you needed to wake up and gain control of your life. You were walking around everyday in a state we'll call *"sleepliving."* You weren't doing what you wanted to do. You had no joy and no passion. You had no sense of direction or purpose. Yes, you were in a state of sleepliving. You were moving from place to place, even accomplishing assigned tasks, but feeling out of touch with what was truly important to you. You had a routine. You got up each day, but you didn't wake up each day fueled to go for it. Actually, you were living a life that was close to empty. You didn't accomplish the dreams, goals, opportunities, and passions that were yours, if only you'd wake up.

What a waste of time, your time, your lifetime! Think for a minute of the changes you could have brought to your world, if you had truly decided to wake up and go for it.

- What things you could have learned…
- What discoveries or inventions you could have accomplished…

- What wonderful relationships you could have had…
- What books, stories, and/or poems you could have written…
- What businesses you could have started…
- What occupations or professions you could have enjoyed and contributed to…
- What mountains, oceans, rivers, and other places you could have explored, *if only you'd chosen to WAKE UP and go for it!*

It is never too late to wake up! What benefits do you really get from the sleepliving state of being? The benefits are much greater when you decide to wake up and live your best life.

What do you have to do in order to WAKE UP?

You have to make the choice and go for it! You might even feel afraid because it will always bring about change. I'll never forget a quotation I heard more than twenty years ago. It stuck with me because I thought, when I heard it, how sad those words were.

> *"The certainty of misery is often better than the misery of uncertainty."*
> Author unknown

We find ourselves certain we're living in misery, lacking joy, just sleepliving in our work, home and/or relationships, yet not making the choice to change. Sleepliving might feel comfortable, but I can assure you that you deserve better! You can't fuel yourself for greatness this way. You have to wake up in order to accomplish greatness.

Okay, are you ready to **WAKE UP** and go for it? It's not hard once you get started. You will get to the point where you never want to waste time in the sleepliving state again. It is time to become more focused and committed, so you can go for all that life has to offer.

Are you ready to get started?

It is important to be intentional about the wake up process.

> *"Intentional acts create extraordinary outcomes!"*
> Dr. Loleta Foster

I want you to follow six steps as you prepare for your wake up call. You will see that the key factors in the steps spell the words WAKE UP! I hope this retention strategy will help you remember the steps in this process. As you read further, you will be encouraged to understand the power of retaining the information you acquire.

Let's do it!

Step 1: What do you **WANT** in life?

You've got to get to the point that you know your wants. Start thinking about what you want – big things, small things, goals, dreams, hopes, relationships, etc. When somebody asks the question, "What do you want?" your response should be, "I am so glad you asked!" Be ready for the opportunity to share what you want, because you know your wants and are excited about them.

Let's practice:
      What do you want?
It's your turn now.
      I'm so glad you asked!

I want _____.

I want _____.

I want _____.

Step 2: What kind of **A**TTITUDE do you demonstrate?

In real estate, it's location, location, location! In life, it's *attitude, attitude, attitude!* Some people just don't get this! You see them letting their attitudes sabotage them in so many aspects of their lives. They often allow other people's behaviors and attitudes to determine their attitudes.

Have you ever gotten up in the morning with all hopes of having a wonderful day and been faced right away with a challenging attitude from someone? Everything was going great and smack in your face is that bad attitude from a family member, co-worker, neighbor or stranger. Here is the challenge. Don't let their bad attitude become contagious. You don't have to catch it! You have a choice about the attitude you demonstrate and maintain. Don't let another person's attitude change you, unless it's for the better!

Is your attitude working for you? Your attitude can be an asset or a liability. You choose! It is so important to check your attitude. Attitude is a powerful thing, and you have to control it. You have to decide to never let your attitude sabotage you as you wake up and go for it. As difficult as it sometimes is to comprehend this, nobody makes us demonstrate a certain attitude. We choose our attitude!

Step 3: What **K**NOWLEDGE do you have to help you do the things you want to do?

You have to invest the time to acquire the knowledge to attain the wants you express. This means you have to spend the necessary time and energy to acquire this knowledge.

What is KNOWLEDGE? Is it different from education or learning? It might be helpful to look at knowledge as acquired information. Now that's pretty broad because we all are exposed to information all the time. So, what do we have to do with acquired information to be able to truly label it as knowledge? Let's consider the following equation for knowledge.

INFORMATION + PROCESSING + RETENTION = KNOWLEDGE

Information alone is the first step, but I do not believe it gives us knowledge. We have to process that information and retain it. I know that you can think of much information that you have been exposed to and processed for a class or task. You may have even retained it until the class was over, the test was taken, or the task was completed. Today, you may remember very little, if anything, of what you retained, but hopefully the acquired knowledge served you well at the time. We have to become motivated to make a commitment to utilize the above equation when we want to successfully attain a desired outcome.

Our local newspaper has an ad campaign that has the message of "Knowledge Changes Everything." When I saw the billboards all over town, I often said to others how much I liked the message. Some months ago, I went to Tampa, Florida to attend a workshop presented by an awesome young man named Delatorro McNeal. One of the first things he focused on during the power-packed workshop was the question of whether knowledge is power. Well, quickly the response by all the participants was, "Yes, knowledge is power!" We felt sure that we had given the right answer, until Del said, "Are you sure knowledge is power?" We responded again, "Yes!" He then asked us to consider the thought that knowledge

alone is not going to change anything, unless it is applied. So, applied knowledge can change everything. Applied knowledge is power! I want to encourage you to consider the following. Knowledge is processed and retained information. That's the first step, but the difference is made when we apply that knowledge:

KNOWLEDGE + APPLICATION = THE POWER TO CHANGE

What would you like to change? You have to start with the knowledge equation we discussed earlier. Once you have the knowledge, what strategies will you develop and use to bring about the desired changes?

Step 4: What are your **ENERGY** sources and levels?

For more than twenty years, I enjoyed driving a vehicle that required diesel fuel. This caused me to look for service stations that sold diesel fuel, because I could not count on every station having it. I had to be more intentional about watching my fuel level, so that I would not find myself out of fuel on my journey.

It is just as important for us to know what fuels us. It is also important to know what level of fueling we should maintain to perform most effectively. From the brief list below, select some of your primary fueling sources. This list will help you start thinking about your fueling sources.

What fuels you?

____ service to others   ____ daydreaming
____ reading   ____ interactions with others
____ time alone   ____ work/job/career
____ gardening   ____ giving
____ drama and conflict   ____ teaching
____ physical activity   ____ writing
____ spiritual activity   ____ competitive games
____ long distance driving   ____ other _____

Now that you are thinking about your fueling sources, how do you make sure you commit to adding enough of these sources to maintain the level of energy you need to accomplish the things you want to accomplish in your life? You have to be honest with yourself about the price you pay when you live in a low energy state. It is important to be aware if you are losing/wasting energy or doing things that sabotage your ultimate goals.

Step 5: Do you know how to **UTILIZE** the things around you?

Learning to utilize things is a powerful tool as you strive to live a life filled with extraordinary outcomes. Before you can make the most of the resources around you, you have to recognize them. There are many categories of resources, for example, human, financial, educational, spiritual, social, emotional, and physical.

How comfortable are you with utilizing the resources available to you? Many of these resources are free for the asking. You will have to be willing to risk reaching out and trying things that will help you attain your goals.

Step 6: Have you developed your power of **PERSISTENCE?**

I have seen many people who have acquired all of the previously mentioned steps and still fallen short of accomplishing their goals. They knew what they wanted and had good attitudes. They put the time and effort into acquiring the necessary knowledge. They kept their energy levels up by fueling themselves for their journey towards greatness, and they utilized the resources around them. What they didn't do was continue to persist until the finish line. It's important to start the race well, maintaining effective strategies as we go, but it's just as important to finish well. To finish well requires persistence. It's true that many things can get in the way, but to go for it means just that, continuing until you get it.

Think of things, during your lifetime, that you could have accomplished, had you demonstrated the power of persistence. It is not enough to see the finish line; you have to cross the finish line. You might become discouraged because the finish line is further away than you thought. You might become frustrated because others reached the finish line faster or with fewer obstacles. It's important to remember that this is your finish line and others' timetables and paths might be very different.

Persistence is that powerful final step in the wake up process. Your persistence factor comes from deep inside you and is controlled by you. It is one of the greatest gifts you can develop and give to yourself!

You now have the steps to acquire your best life, the life you deserve. You have to decide whether you will answer your call!

Get ready! Here it comes.

"Hello, this is your WAKE UP call. I hope you will not continue your sleepliving because an extraordinary life is waiting for YOU!"

Chapter Summary

☐ Knowing what you want and why you want it is key to making the necessary commitments to GO FOR IT!

☐ Intentional acts can create the outcomes you want!

☐ Information + Processing + Retention = Knowledge
Knowledge + Application = The Power to Change!

☐ In life, it's attitude, attitude, attitude! You can have all the necessary ingredients for attaining your goals, but an attitude problem will almost always sabotage extraordinary outcomes.

☐ No one can push you into waking up and going for it, no matter how much they want you to succeed. To WAKE UP and go for it is your choice!

Final Thoughts

Congratulations, you have now been Fueled by Greatness!

You have finished this amazing book, and for that I want to extend to you a hearty, well done! I am certain that by now your brain is on overload with all of the lifework and destiny-shaping that you have done throughout this project. **I know that your dreams, goals, visions, aspirations, and motives have been challenged in a new and renewing way.** I trust that you have participated in the various activities that the chapter authors requested that you participate in, and you have gleaned a tremendous amount of new inspiration, revelation, impartation, and motivation to **make your dreams a living, breathing, rewarding, contributing reality.**

My personal and professional challenge to you is this. Don't let the learning stop here! **Each of these wonderful authors have additional resources in the form of books, tapes, CDs, DVDs, training systems, coaching programs, eNewsletters, articles, live seminars, boot camps, consulting services, and keynotes that are specifically designed to further enhance, enrich, and empower you to manifest the greatness that exists within.** I challenge you to visit each website, click around, and educate yourself on the plethora of products and services that these speakers, authors, and trainers have to offer. **Remember to continue to invest in yourself.** Never stop reading books, attending seminars, listening to motivational material, and growing your life.

It has been a personal pleasure of mine to watch this amazing book take shape, and it is even more of a pleasure to connect with you, yes you, the reader; because you are the reason why we all came together to create this project. We believe in you and your success, and we want you to walk in the power of who God designed and engineered you to be. **So go forth, live the dream,** and know that we, the authors of *Fueled by Greatness,* are somewhere around the world transforming lives and **believing in you and your greatness!**

Living Life Full-Throttle,

Delatorro L. McNeal, II
CEO of Delatorro Worldwide Empowerment
Creator of Fueled by Greatness

Calling All Aspiring
Professional Speakers and Authors!

Do you have a dream of becoming a PAID Professional Speaker? Have you always wanted to publish inspirational and motivational books, or create and sell your own educational learning materials? Have you ever witnessed a speaker on stage and said within yourself, "I would love to do that for a living!"? Have you ever dreamed of owning your own business, traveling the country, and impacting lives with your message, personal story, and life lessons?

If the answer to these questions is yes; than you need to pursue your passion by investing in yourself and your dream. Come spend three life-changing, destiny-shaping, purpose-defining, and career-altering days with Delatorro L. McNeal, II. 90% of the graduates from Delatorro's Boot Camp become professional speakers and published authors in less than a year!

Each of the co-authors of this great book has one very powerful thing in common. They each are graduates of Delatorro's Three Day Professional Speaker and Author Training Boot Camp. They all catapulted into their speaking and publishing greatness, by attending the Boot Camp and participating in Delatorro's Mentorship Program for Speakers and Authors. To learn more about Delatorro's Speaker and Author Training Boot Camps visit us online at www.DelMcNeal.com.

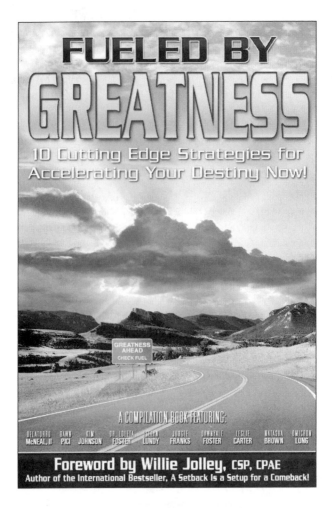

FUELED BY
GREATNESS
10 Cutting Edge Strategies for
Accelerating Your Destiny Now!

A COMPILATION BOOK FEATURING:

DELATORRO   DAWN   KIM   DR. LOLETA   EVELYN   JORGIE   DAWNYALE   LESLIE   NATASHA   OMICRON
McNEAL, II   PICI   JOHNSON   FOSTER   LUNDY   FRANKS   FOSTER   CARTER   BROWN   LONG

Foreword by Willie Jolley, CSP, CPAE
Author of the International Bestseller, A Setback Is a Setup for a Comeback!

To Order Discounted Bulk Quantities of

Fueled by Greatness:
10 Cutting Edge Strategies for Accelerating
Your Destiny Now!

Contact the author from whom you received
this copy.